ABU DHABI
POCKET GUIDE

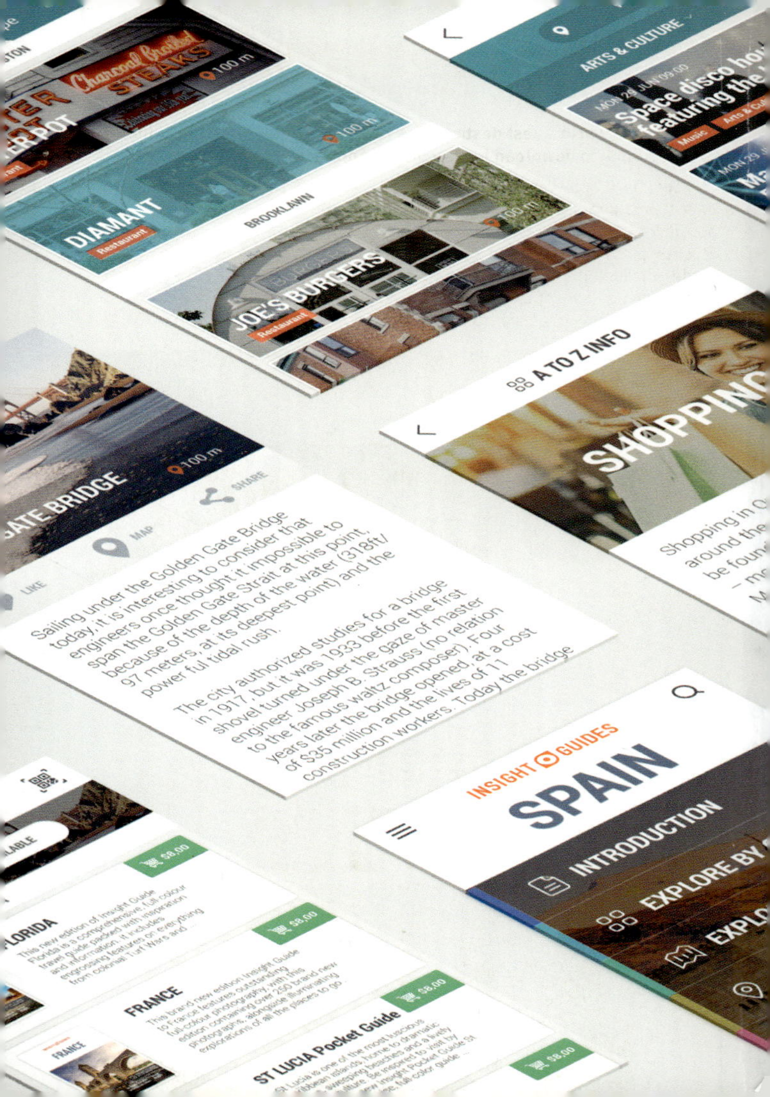

Charcoal Broiled
STEAKS
100 m
DIAMANT
Restaurant
100 m
BROOKLAWN
JOE'S BURGERS
Restaurant
100 m
ARTS & CULTURE
MON 29 JUN 09:00
Music
A TO Z INFO
100 m
SHARE
MAP
LIKE
Sailing under the Golden Gate Bridge today, it is interesting to consider that engineers once thought it impossible to span the Golden Gate Strait at this point, because of the depth of the water (318ft/97 meters, at its deepest point) and the power ful tidal rush.
The city authorized studies for a bridge in 1917, but it was 1933 before the first shovel turned under the gaze of master engineer Joseph B. Strauss (no relation to the famous waltz composer). Four years later the bridge opened, at a cost of $35 million and the lives of 11 construction workers. Today the bridge
INSIGHT GUIDES
SPAIN
INTRODUCTION
$8.00
$8.00
FRANCE
This brand new edition Insight Guide to France features outstanding full-colour photography, with this edition containing over 250 brand new photographs, alongside illuminating explorations of all the places to go.
$8.00
ST LUCIA Pocket Guide
$8.00

Discover the world's best destinations with the Insight Guides Walking Eye app, available to download for free in the App Store and Google Play.

The container app provides easy access to fantastic free content on events and activities taking place in your current location or chosen destination, with the possibility of booking, as well as the regularly-updated Insight Guides travel blog: Inspire Me. In addition, you can purchase curated, premium destination guides through the app, which feature local highlights, hotel, bar, restaurant and shopping listings, an A to Z of practical information and more. Or purchase and download Insight Guides eBooks straight to your device.

INSIGHT GUIDES

Walking Eye

DESTINATIONS

INSPIRE ME

EBOOKS

EVENTS

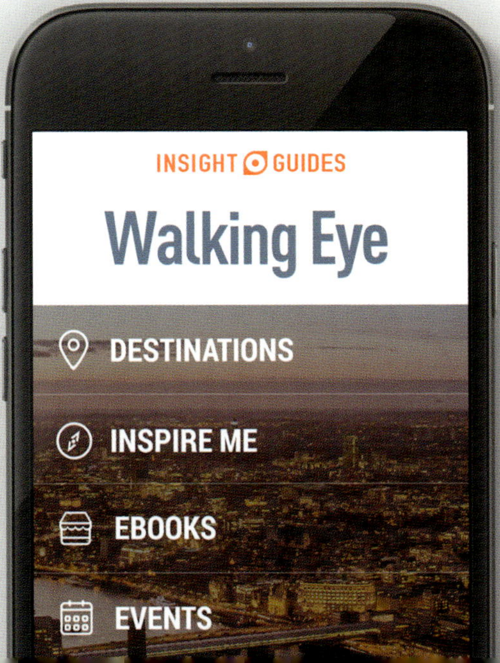

TOP 10 ATTRACTIONS

LIWA SAND DUNES

Liwa Oasis is surrounded by giant sand dunes that slowly change colour throughout the day. See page 63.

NATIONAL AUTO MUSEUM

A marvellous private collection of cars and giant vehicles belonging to the 'Rainbow Sheikh'. See page 50.

SHEIKH ZAYED GRAND MOSQUE

Take a free tour of this magnificent mosque. See page 37.

THE CORNICHE

Stroll along the paths and gardens of the curving waterfront between the turquoise sea and the dramatic city skyline. See page 31.

EMIRATES PALACE HOTEL

Have a look around one of the most expensive and luxurious hotels in the world. See page 27.

AL AIN NATIONAL MUSEUM

See artefacts excavated from ancient sites and learn about Emirati traditions. See page 52.

AL AIN OASIS

Relax to the sounds of trickling water and birdsong in these palm plantations at the heart of Al Ain. See page 53.

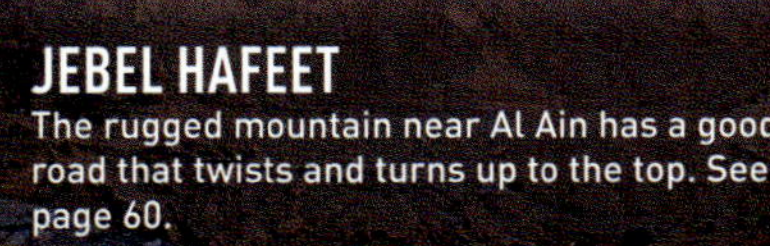

JEBEL HAFEET

The rugged mountain near Al Ain has a good road that twists and turns up to the top. See page 60.

JAHILI FORT

The largest of the restored forts in Al Ain now hosts exhibitions, concerts and a visitor centre. See page 55.

SIR BANI YAS ISLAND

Adventure and luxury on an animal reserve that was originally established in 1971 by Sheikh Zayed bin Sultan al-Nahyan. See page 76.

A PERFECT DAY

8.00am

Breakfast

Energise yourself with the wide choice of foods from the breakfast buffet at your hotel, perhaps sampling a couple of local specialities like ful medames or luqaimat.

10.00am

Grand Mosque

Grab a taxi to the beautiful Sheikh Zayed Grand Mosque and take the free guided tour.

12 noon

Spa treatment

Drive across the Al-Maqtaa Bridge past the famous watchtower and onto the mainland, for a revitalising CHI spa treatment at the Shangri-La Hotel.

1.30pm

Lunch in Qaryat al-Beri

Take an *abra* water taxi along the canal through the Shangri-La resort for lunch in one of the restaurants in the Qaryat al-Beri complex.

3.00pm

Retail therapy

Immerse yourself in the decadent architecture, opulent interiors and regular exhibitions at the Emirates Palace. Then head over to the Breakwater for some retail therapy at Marina Mall, one of the city's largest shopping malls.

5.00pm

Café culture

Have coffee and cake at the lively Havana Café overlooking the marina and Corniche, just across from the main entrance to Marina Mall. You can also consider joining in with the locals and order a *shisha* pipe.

6.00pm

Stroll or cycle along the Corniche

Work off some of the calories with a stroll or cycle ride along the Corniche, while watching the gymnastic water displays of the jet-skiers as they spin and spray their way along the waterfront. Rehydrate with a fruit juice from one of the vendors.

7.30pm

Sunset drink

Pre-dinner drinks at one of Abu Dhabi's many bars with great sea views, such as the Yacht Club at the Intercontinental Hotel.

8.00pm

Dinner with a view

Have dinner in the sky and watch the city life below. The Tiara restaurant high above the Marina Mall revolves every 90 minutes.

10.00pm

Trendy bars

Spend the rest of the night at a lively pub, bar or nightclub, such as the Brauhaus at the Beach Rotana or The Captain's Arms at Le Méridien. For live music, check in at the Hilton's Jazz Bar.

CONTENTS

Features

INTRODUCTION

Abu Dhabi is the largest of the seven emirates that make up the United Arab Emirates (UAE) stretching along the Arabian Gulf coastline of eastern Arabia. In addition to the vibrant modern city of Abu Dhabi, the emirate also boasts spectacular mountains and oases at Al Ain near the border with Oman, and endless sand dunes around Liwa in the south near Saudi Arabia.

A HARSH ENVIRONMENT

With an area of 67,340 sq km (26,000 sq miles), the emirate of Abu Dhabi is slightly smaller than Scotland and accounts for roughly 86 percent of the UAE. The majority of its people live and work in Abu Dhabi City, which is situated on an island slightly smaller than Manhattan just off the coast in the northeast of the emirate. Outside the city's modern air-conditioned high-rises is one of the world's harshest environments. Temperatures can rise above 48°C (118°F), and some areas receive less than 6mm (0.23ins) of rainfall annually. Most of the land is dry undulating desert, with some sand-dune areas in the south and isolated salt flats along the coast. There is a stark beauty to the sand dunes in the southern areas, with great scope for 4x4 desert adventures, and many of the magnificent beaches along the coast are almost untouched.

National flag

The four colours of the UAE flag (red, green, white and black) are the Pan-Arab colours, with the vertical red band symbolising unity. To remember the three horizontal bands think: 'black oil, under white sand, below green palm trees'.

In such a harsh climate, life only exists in places where there is a permanent water supply. Abu Dhabi's water supply comes as a result of a strange geological feature. The whole Arabian plateau is tilted from the west to the east, so that rain falling on the high mountains of Yemen beside the Red Sea slowly flows through aquifers below the Arabian Desert and reappears again some 40,000 years later in the oases of eastern and southeastern Arabia. This natural water source supplies Qatar, Bahrain and all of the Emirates. None of them could have developed in antiquity without it.

Skyscrapers in Abu Dhabi City

TRANSFORMING THE LANDSCAPE

Though at first glance the landpscapes of the country may appear wild and untouched, the hand of man has played an important role. The beautiful lush palm plantations around the oases at Al Ain only exist thanks to water carried in manmade channels known as *falaj*, which were created by some of the area's earliest inhabitants.

Study any photographs of Abu Dhabi City from the 1960s and the changes that have happened since the discovery of oil are quite astounding. What was once a barren desert island has been transformed by massive roadside and parkland irrigation systems into a lush, green paradise. The lack of suitable land to develop was easily resolved by the construction of towering skyscrapers and by reclaiming additional land from the sea, including Lulu Island, the Breakwater and much of the 'downtown' end of the island.

Spectating at the horse-racing is a popular pastime

Yet what you see now is only the beginning of the ongoing development of the city. Plans for the future are even more spectacular. The remarkable Saadiyat Island development is set to feature Arabian off-shoots of the prestigious Louvre and Guggenheim museums (both due to open in 2017), while the Masdar City complex out near the airport aims to create the world's first carbon-neutral city, placing Abu Dhabi firmly in the vanguard of the region's cultural and technological development.

TRADITIONAL AND MODERN LIFESTYLES

In many Arab countries there is a sense of remorse for the broken ties with seasonal desert life and the associated traditions of family life, livestock and tribal village. Here in Abu Dhabi modernisation has been so swift and dramatic that those traditional lifestyles are very much within living memory. Many of the older generation grew up following daily rituals that had remained unchanged for hundreds of years, at a time when the journey from Abu Dhabi Island to Al Ain took five days by camel. The younger generations have since had an upbringing far removed from these times. Such rapid changes are set to continue.

However, unlike most other Middle Eastern countries, where people are faced with a tough choice between a rural life of relative poverty and the better prospects of living in a town or city, Abu Dhabians can have the best of both worlds. An impressive road-construction programme has joined the desert and the city, now just a short air-conditioned car journey away. Many families now maintain homes in both the city and the desert, keeping one eye on the future, while retaining important links with the past.

According to the 2015 statistics published by the Abu Dhabi Statistics Centre there are 506,411 Abu Dhabi nationals, but the emirate is also home to about four times that number of ex-pat workers. The rate of migration into Abu Dhabi is one of the highest in the world and, when combined with one of the world's lowest death rates, gives Abu Dhabi a high average annual population growth rate of 9.5 per cent (2005–2014).

Most of the migrant labour force recruited to build the emirate comes from the nearby Indian subcontinent, but there are also service-industry personnel and construction workers from across the Arab world, all bringing cultural diversity to Abu Dhabi. The emirate is home to thousands of Westerners attracted by the constant flow of new corporate, financial and engineering projects, and keen to bring up their young families in a safe, affluent environment.

HOW ABU DHABI GOT ITS NAME

It seems that the original name of the island where Abu Dhabi City now stands was *milh* (meaning 'salt'), perhaps referring to the salty water or salt deposits. This mineral, together with the freshwater springs, attracted wildlife, particularly gazelles *(dhabi)*.

According to tribal folklore, in 1761 a Bani Yas hunting party from Liwa followed gazelle tracks across the shallows onto the island where the animal was found drinking at a natural spring. When this was reported back to Sheikh Dhiab bin Isa in Liwa, he ordered that a village should be established near the freshwater spring. Bedouins originally called the island Umm Dhabi (mother of the gazelle) but the British renamed it Abu Dhabi (father of the gazelle).

The tempting sea and peaceful beach at Jebel Dhanna on the western coast

A SUSTAINABLE FUTURE

Thanks to Sheikh Zayed bin Sultan al-Nahyan's guiding influence, who ruled the emirate from 1966 until 2004, Abu Dhabi's expansion has followed a more measured and sustainable path than some of its neighbours. Rather than seeking 'quick fixes', every aspect of development has been carefully planned.

In particular, changes have been made with great consideration for the delicate balance of both desert and marine environments – the very basis of everything that Sheikh Zayed stood for. An excellent illustration of this principle is Sir Bani Yas Island, established by Sheikh Zayed as a nature reserve in 1971. Over time the island has been transformed from a dusty desert to a lush savannah, with several million trees planted and thousands of free-roaming animals introduced. Other examples include the huge Shams 1, an enormous solar-energy plant, opened in 2013.

Abu Dhabi has the unique opportunity, and the resources, to develop at a pace like nowhere else. With the guiding principles of Sheikh Zayed in mind, it is certain to continue to do so.

A BRIEF HISTORY

Although the United Arab Emirates was only formed after independence from the British in 1971, there is evidence that the area has been inhabited since the early Stone Age. One of the problems in tracing Abu Dhabi's past is that for a long time its history was only recalled through oral tribal traditions. Archaeological research is now in full flow, and every season brings new discoveries, filling great gaps in the timeline.

The first *Homo sapiens* came to southern Arabia from Africa, and then passed through what is now Yemen and Oman. The earliest evidence of human occupation of the emirate is stone tools dating from about 150,000 years ago, found at Jebel Barakah west of Jebel Dhanna. At this time climatic conditions in the region are believed to have been considerably cooler and wetter than they are today.

Around 10,000 years ago nomads roaming the Arabian and Syrian deserts gradually settled at suitable sites alongside the Tigris and Euphrates rivers, and early Mesopotamian civilisations such as the Sumerians and Babylonians began to develop. However, the area lacked metal ores, so the Sumerians sailed their primitive craft on intrepid journeys around the Gulf to trade with the Indus Valley states of Mohenjodaro and Harappa (in what is now Pakistan), using every suitable coastal inlet for protection. Maritime trade settlements formed in areas with reliable water supplies.

Gold pendant dating from the Wadi Suq period

A carving on the Bronze Age Grand Tomb at Hili

These colonies along the creeks, islands, headlands and peninsulas eventually became Qatar, Bahrain and the Emirates.

EARLY PERIODS

A sizeable coastal community seems to have been established by the Neolithic period. On the island of Marawah the skeleton of a man aged between 20 and 40 was found buried on a stone platform within a larger building dated to 7,500 years ago. Similar Ubaid-period (5500–3800BC) house structures have been found on Dalma Island to the west, uncovered along with beads, flints and imported pottery. However, human activity at this time was not restricted to coastal areas, and 7,000-year-old Neolithic settlements with stone tools have been found in the deserts southeast of Liwa Oasis.

Several distinct cultures developed in the area over the course of the Bronze Age (3200–1200BC). The earliest is the Hafeet culture, typified by the ancient tombs with bronze funerary objects found near Al Ain. The slightly later Umm an-Nar culture is characterised by larger, multi-chambered tombs, several of which can be seen in the Archaeological Park at Hili. It is thought that Hili may have been part of the copper-producing region referred to by the Sumerians as 'Magan'. Copper ore from the nearby Omani mountains may have been smelted at Hili and exported from a port on Umm an-Nar Island (after which the culture is named) on the edge of Abu Dhabi city, where similar tombs and artefacts have been found. The later Wadi Suq culture is characterised by the long narrow tombs and wonderful gold and silver animal figure pendants found at Al Qatara.

As imported iron replaced copper during the 1st millennium BC, the old copper-working centres of Arabia seem to have been abandoned. By this time the domestication of the camel had improved desert trade and communication, and the population became semi-nomadic, moving their herds of animals with the seasons. This period also heralded one of the region's greatest inventions – the *falaj* irrigation system (see box). Increased food production in well-watered places such as at the base of mountains led to a rise in population in these areas. Along the coast,

THE FALAJ SYSTEM

As the first settlements developed in the Abu Dhabi region, the most precious commodity was water, which often had to be brought in from nearby mountains. Around 3,000 years ago the *falaj* (plural *aflaj*) system was introduced to improve water supplies. Underground channels were dug by hand to carry the water, thus reducing evaporation. Vertical shafts were dug for ventilation and to remove silt and stones brought down the channel. The use of this system spread around neighbouring regions, and it is still unclear if it originated in Arabia or Persia (where they are known as *qanats*). The best ancient examples are found around Al Ain.

Because *aflaj* were so vital to life in these inhospitable areas, they had to be protected by watchtowers. An entire settlement could easily be defeated by cutting its water supply. The job of digging and repairing a *falaj* is highly skilled, requiring nerve and agility to work underground in small tunnels full of dust.

small fishing communities practised seasonal pearl-diving to supplement their meagre incomes.

From the 3rd century BC the region came under the control of the Greeks as they pushed eastwards through Asia. During this time there is evidence that the Aramaic language was spoken and written, and coins were minted at Mleiha, just across the modern border in Sharjah. The Romans regularly traded with India through the Gulf: Pliny the Younger mentions Mleiha in the 1st century AD, when several ports appear to have been operating along the Emirati coast. The next major influence was the Sassanians based across the Gulf in Persia, who fought both the Romans and the Arabs. During this period, early Christian communities sought isolation, as shown by the Nestorian monasteries found on Sir Bani Yas and Marawah islands.

ARRIVAL OF ISLAM

AD570 was a momentous year in Arabia, marked by the birth of the Prophet Mohammed in Mecca, as well as the collapse of the Great Dam at Marib in southern Arabia. The ancestors of Abu Dhabi's ruling family were among the many Arabs who fled Marib and eventually settled in the Abu Dhabi region. Islam spread around Arabia along the desert and sea-trade routes, and the scattered desert and coastal communities of Abu Dhabi were quick to adopt the new religion.

As the centre of Islamic control moved eastwards with the Umayyids of Damascus and then the Abbasids of Baghdad, the Gulf rose in international significance. During Abbasid rule, trade along the coast from Basra stretched as far as the East Indies and even China. Tentative research has shown important Abbasid-era houses in northern Abu Dhabi and perhaps an Abbasid mosque at Al Ain. However, when Islamic power shifted west towards Cairo during the Fatimid

Al Hosn Fort, built in 1795, is now surrounded by skyscrapers

era and then to Constantinople under the Ottomans, the Gulf once again lost its importance, until the rise of Shi'a Islam in Persia during the 16th century.

Under the Safavids of Isfahan, the Gulf ports became important commercial centres for trade with emerging European powers such as the Portuguese, Dutch and British, who also purchased local pearls along the Emirati coast. With such riches being transported just off the coast, the natural inlets and secure anchorages of Abu Dhabi now acted as perfect hideaways for those who plundered the European ships.

DESERT TRIBES AND THE TRUCIAL COAST

Long a centre for desert dwellers, the fertile crescent of Liwa Oasis became a stronghold of the Bani Yas tribe in the late 15th century. A Bani Yas hunting party are said to have discovered the island that would become Abu Dhabi in 1761 by following wild gazelle tracks to a spring (see page 13). Around 1795 Sheikh Shakhbut bin Dhiab moved the centre of Bani Yas

Pearl-diving in the Persian Gulf, 1870

power from Liwa to Abu Dhabi, building the Al-Hosn Fort to serve as his base and to protect the valuable water source.

In the late 18th century tribal territories began to take the shape of the present Emirates. Liwa, Buraimi/Al Ain and Abu Dhabi were under the control of the Bani Yas tribe, while the Al Bu Falasahs controlled Dubai, and Sharjah and Ras al-Khaimah were strongholds of the powerful Al-Qawasim tribe.

The strategic importance of the Gulf as a staging post en route to India was meanwhile assuming increasing importance, and in 1853 the British signed a series of agreements, or 'truces', with all the local rulers in what subsequently became known as the Trucial States, the forerunner of the modern UAE. These peaceful times of the mid-19th century allowed pearl-fishing along the Trucial Coast to develop into a major industry. Dalma Island became the centre of the pearling industry, and Abu Dhabi exported the best pearls in the world.

Some members of the Bani Yas tribe spent the winters on Abu Dhabi Island and the hot summers in the cooling shade of the watered oases at Buraimi/Al Ain and Liwa. One of the main reasons why Abu Dhabi is the dominant force within the Emirates goes back to 1868, when Sheikh Zayed bin Khalifa (Sheikh Zayed the First) killed the Al-Qawasim ruler of Sharjah in hand-to-hand fighting.

However, once again the Gulf became sidelined as the opening of the Suez Canal in 1869 shifted emphasis across to the Red Sea. The development of the steamship also allowed larger ships to bypass the Gulf and head directly across the Indian Ocean to India. At around the same time a strengthening of Shi'a Islam in Persia forced many coastal Sunni Persians across the Gulf into Arabia, bringing with them their shipping and trade contacts, especially Indian merchants who took the valuable Gulf pearls direct to India.

THE OIL YEARS

After ruling for over 50 years, Sheikh Zayed the First died in 1907. After a series of family feuds, in 1928 Sheikh Shakhbut bin Sultan al-Nahyan took control. During this time, Abu Dhabi was spared many of the problems of the World Wars,

FIRST OIL EXPORTS

Offshore exploration for oil in the 1950s and 60s was under the direction of ADMA – Abu Dhabi Marine Areas Ltd, whose oil wells off Das Island produced their first tanker load of oil in 1962. On 4 July the BP-owned *British Signal* filled up with a quarter of a million barrels of Abu Dhabi crude at the oil-export terminal and set sail for Japan. On 14 December 1963 the first shipment from the onshore field at Bab left Jebel Dhanna port, when the tanker Esso Dublin headed for the refinery at Milford Haven in Wales with almost 34,000 tons of crude, roughly the same amount as in the first shipment from Das.

but the Great Depression and Japan's development of the cultured pearl virtually ended the local pearling industry. Other Emirates and Gulf States such as Bahrain, Qatar and Kuwait signed oil agreements with British or American companies in the 1930s, and many Abu Dhabians moved to work there. Further instability was caused by border disputes with Dubai in 1945 and the problem of the Buraimi/Al Ain Oasis, which was claimed by Abu Dhabi, Oman and Saudi Arabia. According to Wilfred Thesiger, the population of Abu Dhabi Island in the late 1940s had dwindled to around 2,000 hardy souls struggling to survive in *barasti* huts built of palm fronds, few of whom stayed there all year. The entire population of Abu Dhabi Emirate was only about 13,000, even in the late 1950s.

Oil exploration concessions had been in place in Abu Dhabi both onshore and offshore since the 1930s, but it was not until 1959 that sufficient reserves were discovered at Murban, within the Bab oilfield, 100km (60 miles) southwest of Abu Dhabi Island. Das Island, 180km (110 miles) offshore, began production in 1962 and Bab finally came online the following year.

A great leader

Sheikh Zayed bin Sultan al-Nahyan's reign encompassed his country's seamless transition from a poor colonial tribal state to a successful modern international nation. As a young man he learnt how to hunt in the desert using falcons and saluki dogs. Some expeditions lasted for several weeks and involved riding camels for hundreds of kilometres.

Sheikh Shakhbut was wary of dealing with British companies and hesitant about agreeing to major expansion. His main concern was the uncertainty that his tiny percentage of oil revenues would continue to flow and that sufficient cash reserves should be held for emergencies, such as further border disputes. However, the youngest of his brothers, Sheikh Zayed bin Sultan al-Nahyan, felt that this was unnecessarily holding back Abu Dhabi's development. Family negotiations led to Sheikh Zayed becoming ruler of Abu Dhabi on 6 August 1966, as Sheikh Shakhbut retired to Bahrain, finally dying in Al Ain in 1989.

Painting of Sheikh Zayed at Al Ain Palace Museum

UNITING THE ARAB EMIRATES

In 1968 the British announced their intention to withdraw their military presence from the Gulf, leaving the Emirates vulnerable to outside interference. Burying old differences and under the leadership of Sheikh Zayed, the Trucial States came together to form the United Arab Emirates on 2nd December 1971, with Sheikh Zayed as President.

Almost immediately this new federation had to transform itself from a collection of minor tribal societies into a modern government with national institutions and public services. Everything was created from scratch, from medical and educational facilities to police and security forces, all paid for with oil revenues. Sheikh Zayed's remarkable vision meant that all Abu Dhabians were involved in the great wave of expansion, with free land on offer and financial support available to establish local businesses.

An agreement in 1974 with Saudi Arabia finally resolved the Buraimi land dispute in favour of Abu Dhabi, but at the cost

On-shore oil in Abu Dhabi

of losing a stretch of coastline in the far west, giving the Saudis the entire border with Qatar. Further regional stability was assured when Abu Dhabi joined other Gulf countries by establishing the Gulf Co-operation Council (GCC) in 1981.

With its reliance on petroleum, the economy surged and stuttered through the 1980s as the oil price rose and fell. Gradually a modern infrastructure was put in place, accompanied by the first efforts to diversify away from oil. The skyline of the city has reflected these changes as office and residential skyscrapers have pushed the profile of the crowded downtown area steadily upwards.

Abu Dhabi has continued to develop under Sheikh Khalifa, since his father Sheikh Zayed died on 2 November 2004. The emirate is now one of the main players in the GCC economic alliance and an ever more important business hub between Europe, Asia and Africa. The city is increasingly looking to diversify away from an economy still largely centred on oil, with ongoing initiatives including the stunning Saadiyat Island museums and the remarkable Masdar development, intended to become the world's first carbon-neutral city. The emergence of Abu Dhabi as a major cultural destination and world leader in green technology is one that few people would have predicted even 10 years ago, while the future is likely to provide many further and equally dramatic surprises.

HISTORICAL LANDMARKS

***c*.5500BC** Traders stop along the coast en route to the Indian Ocean.

***c*.3200BC** Bronze Age settlements and copper trade around Al Ain.

***c*.2700BC** Umm al-Nar culture; large burial tombs at Hili.

***c*.1000BC** *Falaj* system of underground water channels developed.

3rd century BC Greeks influence Gulf trade, followed by Romans.

6th century AD Nestorian monasteries founded on Sir Bani Yas and Marawah islands.

7th century AD Islam spreads throughout the Arabian Peninsula.

15th century Liwa Oasis becomes the base of the Bani Yas tribe.

1761 Legendary settling of Abu Dhabi Island by the Bani Yas tribe.

1795 Building of the Al-Hosn Fort by Sheikh Shakhbut bin Dhiab.

1820 Initial treaty between Britain and the coastal tribes.

1853 Final peace treaty between British and the Emirati sheikhs.

1855 Sheikh Zayed the First begins a rule lasting over 50 years.

1907 Death of Sheikh Zayed the First.

1928 Sheikh Shakhbut bin Sultan al-Nahyan takes control.

1935 First oil agreement signed with the British.

1948 Wilfred Thesiger arrives in Liwa after crossing the desert by camel.

1959 Major oil reserves discovered at the Bab oilfield.

1962 First shipment of Abu Dhabi crude oil from Das Island.

1966 Sheikh Zayed bin Sultan al-Nahyan becomes ruler.

1971 Formation of the UAE, with Sheikh Zayed as the first president.

1974 Resolution of the rival claims on Buraimi Oasis settled.

1981 Gulf Co-operation Council (GCC) formed.

1995 Abu Dhabi and UAE join the World Trade Organization.

2004 Death of Sheikh Zayed; Sheikh Khalifa becomes president.

2009 First F1 Grand Prix held at Yas Island.

2010 Opening of the first phase of Masdar City.

2013 Opening of the Shams 1 solar power plant.

2017 Planned opening of the Guggenheim and Louvre museums, Saadiyat Island.

WHERE TO GO

Abu Dhabi City is located on an island just off the mainland. The densely packed downtown area is at the western end, between Haza bin Zayed Street and the Corniche. Here you will find the greatest choice of hotels, restaurants and shops. To the east is the mainly residential uptown area, where three bridges connect the island with the city's suburbs on the mainland. The best way to get around is by taxi or the bus system. Almost everything in the city has been created in the last few decades, so to catch a glimpse of earlier times venture out into the rest of the emirate – east to the town of Al Ain, south to Liwa Oasis and west to the expanses of Al Gharbia. Hiring a car is the best way to do this, or a 4x4 for a real adventure.

DOWNTOWN ABU DHABI

Only three generations ago the western end of Abu Dhabi island was a beach fringed by a few *barasti* palm-frond fishermen's huts. Today it is home to some of the world's most expensive real estate and cutting-edge buildings designed by world-class architects. The Corniche is the natural focus of the area, stretching 8km (5 miles) along the northwestern seafront.

EMIRATES PALACE HOTEL

The southern end of the Corniche begins at the headland of **Al-Ras al-Akhdar**, dominated by two huge enclosures – the Presidential Palace and the Emirates Palace Hotel.

The **Emirates Palace Hotel** ❶ is built to the highest specifications on an epic Hollywood scale, and is without doubt one of the planet's most grandiose and opulent places to stay.

Modern skyscrapers and traditional houses sit alongside each other in downtown Abu Dhabi

Remarkably, it is also open to any visitor who wants to come in and look around. It may seem strange to visit a hotel as a tourist attraction, but the Emirates Palace is no ordinary hotel, as the $3 billion price tag might indicate. The statistics are staggering – marble imported from 13 countries; over 1,000 chandeliers; 8,000 trees planted and beach sand from Algeria.

The massive **gateway** running from the roundabout at the end of Bainunah Street (34th Street) is only used for top-end VIPs – presidents and major leaders. The ramp runs straight up to a private reception area on the fifth floor, avoiding the main check-in area downstairs. The closer one gets, the more impressive its detail and scale, until eventually stepping inside and passing reception. The **atrium** is simply mind-blowing with its size, colour and layout. Tiers of golden balconies reach up to the latticed golden octagon supporting the grand dome, over 70m (230ft) from the marble flooring.

There are more reasons to come here than simply to marvel at the decor. With the current lack of museum space in the city, the hotel's public areas also serve as venues for world-class history, art and culture **exhibitions**; anything from Picasso paintings to religious bronzes. See www.emiratespalace.com for current exhibition details. The 1,100-seater **auditorium** and outside **concert area** for 20,000 spectators have already attracted internationally renowned artists including Elton John, Coldplay and George Michael. Needless to say, a meal or drink here is not cheap, but it is certainly memorable. Outside, the hotel's **private beach**

Emirates Palace Hotel

Admiring the view from the end of the Breakwater

stretches 1.4km (1 mile) around a shallow turquoise bay, connecting the Breakwater development with a small marina.

A short distance to the southeast of the Emirates Palaces sits the **Presidential Palace**, ringed with tight security, while the gargantuan Arabian-style complex currently under construction on the east side of the Emirates Palace is the **New Presidential Palace**, intended to eventually provide a home for the president, crown prince and UAE government.

THE BREAKWATER

East of the Emirates Palace Hotel a road turns past a giant image of Sheikh Zayed and runs along a causeway jutting out into the sea. At the end is the large **Breakwater** development of villas, marinas and shopping outlets.

Dominating the area is the sprawling **Marina Mall ❷**, which has over 400 shopping outlets, nine cinema screens and a 32-lane bowling village, plus countless restaurants and cafés. Soaring up from the back of the mall is the landmark **Burj al**

Marina tower – the Tiara Restaurant (see page 110) at the top of the tower revolves once every 90 minutes, giving wonderful views across the city skyline.

Outside, the lively Havana Café overlooks the **water sports marina** that is home to the Abu Dhabi International Marine Sports Club, a venue for boat races and the sailing training centre. The café has great views along the Breakwater to the Heritage Village and giant national flag perched on the end.

A short walk away, the **Heritage Village** ❸ (Sat–Thur 9am–5pm, Fri 3.30–9pm; free) forms a kind of living museum of Abu Dhabi's traditional past, where the trades and crafts of yesteryear are displayed and explained. Model *dhows* and full-sized fishing boats lie along the pleasant beach beside a replica fort. Local clothing and souvenirs such as perfumes, spices and pottery are sold from village huts and camel-hair tents. The on-site Al-Asalah restaurant

Tourists exploring the Heritage Village

has great views across the lagoon to the Corniche.

Outside is an enormous free-standing **flagpole**, one of the tallest in the world at 122m (400ft). It was erected in 2001 to celebrate the 30th National Day anniversary. Below it is the beautifully decorated **Abu Dhabi Theatre**.

Sunset on the Corniche

THE CORNICHE AND AL-HOSN DISTRICT

Running along the northwest seafront, the broad **Corniche** road is flanked by a long swathe of parkland and a spacious blue-flag beach, well away from the streaming traffic. You can hire a bicycle from various places along the Corniche (see page 116) and ride along the cycle lane or the wide pedestrian walkway all the way to Al Mina. The waters just off the Corniche are sheltered by the enormous manmade Lulu Island, and come alive in the late afternoon with jet-skiers whizzing across the water.

Halfway along the Corniche is the Al-Hosn district, home to the city's oldest buildings. The original whitewashed fort and a few palm trees are a quaint throwback, surrounded as they are by high-rises and skyscrapers. **Al-Hosn Fort** ❹ was constructed around 1795 by the leader of the Bani Yas tribe, Sheikh Shakhbut bin Dhiab, when he moved here permanently from Liwa. It has a typical desert fort layout with four watchtowers and was slightly modernised in the 19th century. The fort remained the seat of government and the official residence of the ruling sheikh until Sheikh

Zayed took control in 1966. The fort is currently undergoing extensive redevelopment and will reopen in the future as a major museum of Emirati history and heritage, although no one as yet seems to know exactly when this will be. The attached **Cultural Foundation**, on Sheikh Zayed the First Street, is also closed pending decisions regarding the building's future.

From here, the main road back to the Corniche passes through **Al-Ittihad Square** ❺ with its giant street sculptures, including a cannon, fort and coffee pot. The area immediately east of the square was formerly home to the largest of the city's various old souks until it burnt down in a disastrous fire in 2004. The old souk has now been replaced by the gleaming **World Trade Center** development, topped by a huge pair of cylindrical skyscrapers known as Trust Tower and The Domain. Far more interesting is the stunning **souk** within, designed by Foster & Partners in a suave, postmodern style blending Arabian and Oriental motifs to memorable effect. Subdued lighting combines with wafts of perfume and spices and huge quantities of latticework wooden panelling. There are also a few interesting craft, food and souvenir shops here, plus a couple of pleasant cafes in the lofty central atrium.

Two blocks east of the Cultural Foundation on the opposite side of Sheikh Zayed the First Street is the **Madinat Zayed Gold Souk** ❻, destination of choice for gold-buyers for decades.

Dhows

In their heyday there were many types of *dhow* built for different purposes. Graceful *baglahs* and *ghanjahs* were typical long-distance ocean-going boats for trading with the Indies, while *sambuqs* and *jalibuts* were smaller, more agile craft, ideal for sailing and pearling in the calmer waters of the Gulf.

Whether you are buying or not, it is interesting to look at the glistening shop windows and intricate workmanship. The surrounding streets contain many older, family-run shops, as well as the central post office and a local shopping centre. Further out are the Al-Wahda Shopping Mall and the main bus station.

The headquarters of the Abu Dhabi Investment Authority

AL-MINA AND THE TOURIST CLUB AREA

At the northern end of the Corniche is **Al Mina ('The Harbour') district**. On the left at this point is a *dhow* harbour and fishing port, the departure point for the Al-Dhafra sunset cruise boat and Al-Mina coffee shop. The local **fish and vegetable souks** ❼ are always lively, and you never know what you will find in the street stalls of the **Iranian Souk**. This was the main shopping area for tourists a decade ago, but the future of the Al Mina area is uncertain as blocks of land are already earmarked for development.

Inland from here is the **Tourist Club Area**, stretching past the beach resorts that have always been popular with tourists and expats for their easy access, safe bathing and lively nightlife. The **Abu Dhabi Mall** ❽ (www.abudhabi-mall.com) is smaller than the Marina Mall, but handily situated in the middle of the Tourist Club Area. In addition to more than 200 shops, it has a cinema, bowling alley and exhibitions area.

The dhow harbour

UPTOWN ABU DHABI

As the island narrows towards the mainland, the roads running along its length are squeezed together until there are just three main highways. Along the northern coast is the Eastern Ring Road (Al-Salam Street), leading to the Sheikh Zayed Bridge, while on the southern side is Coast Road (30th Street), which runs across the large Al-Mussafah Bridge onto the mainland. The main road down the centre of the island is Sheikh Rashid bin Saeed al-Maktoum Road (Old Airport Road), which leads to the famous Al-Maqtaa Bridge.

AL-MUSHRIF

Leaving downtown and heading for **Al Mushrif**, the landscape opens up with quiet residential areas and embassy compounds set along tree-lined avenues. The huge **Abu Dhabi Equestrian Club** is located here, with a training centre, horse-racing track and golf course. Tucked in beside this is the **Abu Dhabi Country Club**, offering a wide range of indoor and outdoor recreation (see page 90).

On the other, eastern side of Al-Karamah Street is the **Church Area**, where the services reflect the diversity of Abu Dhabi's Christian community. **St Andrew's Church** is part of the Diocese of Cyprus and the Gulf and is a centre for Scottish community activities. Next door is the Sheikh Mohammed bin Zayed Mosque, and just around the corner is **St Joseph's Cathedral**, offering daily services in several European and Asian languages. A few streets away is **St George's Cathedral**, the main centre of worship for southern Indian Christians.

Nearby is the **Women's Union and Handicraft Centre** ❾ (Sun–Thur 7am–3pm; tel: 02-447 6645), where local women produce traditional art and craftwork. Some unique handmade pieces are on show and available to buy, including threadwork, weaving, paintings and perfumes. Women can get a variety of henna designs painted on their hands by skilled female artists. The centre is in the Women's Association Complex on Al- Karama St, near the Immigration Office and Royal Stables.

At the northern end of Al-Saada Street is the busy **Eastern Ring Road**, running alongside a **Marine Conservation Area**. Despite being so close to the city, these inter-tidal mudflats are an important habitat for wading birds, as well as protecting the dense mangrove swamps and sea-grass beds, which are full of maturing fish. The

Traditional styles

Whilst Western styles are popular for both men and women, many Emiratis prefer traditional clothing. The white ankle-length robe for men is called a *thawb* (also known as a *dishdasha*) and is loose and practical in the hot temperatures, while some women wear a long black dress called an *abaya*.

coastline here has some great picnic areas with views across the shallow bays to the distant downtown high rises.

Coast Road on the opposite side of the island is just as busy, with long stretches of pleasant pedestrian walkways at the water's edge. The coastline here is more open with less vegetation, offering great views across to the manmade islands and breakwaters.

GRAND MOSQUE AREA

This area at the eastern end of the island will become familiar to you if you spend time at the **Abu Dhabi National Exhibition Centre** (www.adnec.ae), a venue not only for conferences, but also for festivals and sports. Right next to the centre, you cannot fail to notice the extraordinary Capital Gate skyscraper, looking like a postmodern Leaning Tower of Pisa about to topple over onto the traffic below. Built at an incline of eighteen degrees, it has been officially recognized by the Guinness Book of World Records as the 'World's Furthest Leaning Man-Made Tower'.

Sheikh Zayed Grand Mosque

Private charters and smaller planes on internal flights around the emirate use the old **Al-Bateen Airport** nearby.

Zayed Sports City ❿, east of the exhibition centre, offers a whole range of sporting activities, all within a short walk of each other. The main landmark is the huge, white-arched, 55,000-seater **Sheikh Zayed Stadium**, which hosted the FIFA Club World Cup in 2009 and 2010. Nearby is the **International Tennis Complex**, which hosts the annual Mubadala World Tennis Championship, attracting the world's top players. At the end of the car park is the Olympic-sized ice rink, suitable for all levels of skaters through the day and given over to ice hockey in the evenings. Pro-standard bowling is available at the 40-lane Khalifa International Bowling Centre, which also has a number of pool tables.

The Grand Mosque's carpet is the largest in the world

Further east still, the **Sheikh Zayed Grand Mosque** ⓫ (Sat–Thur 9am–10pm, on Fridays from 4.30pm, guided tours free) is one of the largest mosques in the world, and has rapidly established itself as one of the region's leading tourist attractions. From a distance the domes and minarets look like something from *Arabian Nights*, but close up it is the combination of huge scale and minute detail that really impresses. Inspired by some of the greatest Islamic buildings ever created, it is a harmonious blend of Moorish, Mughal and Persian architecture, built by master craftsmen from around the world.

The **courtyard** outside can accommodate 32,000 worshippers, with space for another 9,000 inside the main prayer halls. The swirling green **carpet** is the largest in the world and took two years to weave in the holy city of Mashhad in Iran. Hanging from the 70m (230ft) high central dome is the world's largest

chandelier, made in Germany from 1 million Swarovski crystals. The enormous ***qibla* wall** (which indicates the direction of Mecca) is decorated with the 99 names of Allah in Kufic script, each one illuminated by hidden fibre-optic cables.

The opening of the mosque to non-Muslims was intended to encourage greater understanding of Islam and offers a wonderful opportunity to see high-quality Islamic art and design close up. The whole building is a beautiful interpretation of classical Islamic architecture in the most modern simplistic style. The mosque was inspired by Sheikh Zayed, and, sadly, his funeral was one of the first ceremonies here.

Taking a guided tour of the Grand Mosque

Details of the mosque's opening hours (roughly Sat–Thur 9am–10pm, Fri 4.30–10pm) and regular free ADTA guided tours are posted at www.szgmc.ae/en. Shoes must be removed, and visitors should wear modest, conservative loose-fitting clothing with long sleeves. Shorts and short skirts are not acceptable, and women must cover their heads. Photography is allowed.

On the other side of the Coast Road is the graceful golden roof of the **Armed Forces Officers' Club**. The main building of the Officers' Club is a social complex that also doubles as a hotel; the areas behind reception hold pictorial exhibitions about UAE troops from the times of the Trucial States Defence to the present day. The **Caracal Shooting Club** is based here, where members of the public can let off a few rounds and practise their aim with real bullets or laser beams (see page 90).

The oil-rig tank in Sheikh Khalifa Park's Aquarium

SHEIKH KHALIFA PARK

Sheikh Khalifa Park ⓬ (Sun–Wed 3–10pm, Thur–Sat 10am–11pm) is on the opposite side of Al-Bateen Airport, tucked into a tiny corner of the island. Within the substantial area of landscaped parkland are pools, fountains and children's play areas, popular with families at evenings and weekends. If walking the 1km (0.6 miles) from one end to the other is too much, catch the small train down and back.

The most important historical building in the park is the **Summer Palace of Sheikh Shakhbut**, about halfway down the main drive. It sounds grander than it actually is – a small single-storey set of three rooms, built of rough sandstone blocks, gypsum and palm-tree wood. The only building of its type remaining, it shows the simple lifestyle of Abu Dhabi's ruler only half a century ago.

At the far end of the park is the Khalifa Park **Aquarium**, which has a selection of Gulf fish species and a view of an oil rig on the seabed. In the same building is a gentle computerised **Time Tunnel** ride (additional charge), which takes about twenty minutes to travel past a series of life-size scenes depicting major stages in the history of Abu Dhabi.

ISLANDS AROUND ABU DHABI CITY

One of Abu Dhabi City's greatest current projects is its expansion onto the nearby inshore islands. Some of these are natural, such as Saadiyat and Al-Samaliyah, while others are manmade, including Yas, Reem, Lulu and Horseshoe.

CITY-CENTRE ISLANDS

A cluster of islands rings the end of Abu Dhabi island, facing across to the Corniche and downtown. Connected by a bridge to the Tourist Club Area of downtown, Al Maryah (formerly Sowwah) and Al Reem Islands are the two closest to the city centre, and currently the focus of the most intensive development, with huge skyscrapers rising in every direction. **Al Maryah Island** is intended to become the financial heart of the city, home to the Abu Dhabi Stock

Frank Gehry's design for Saadiyat Island's Guggenheim Museum

Exchange, along with a vast Cleveland Clinic, the city's flagship healthcare project. Just beyond here, massive commercial developments are currently underway on the larger **Al Reem Island**, the first area in the city in which foreign citizens are being allowed to buy property.

Unlike Al Maryah and Al Reem, other central islands remain virtually undeveloped, with no infrastructure and accessible only to people with their own boats – although a fair number of locals come to picnic and camp out on their beaches or to mess around in jet-skis and power-boats on the water (left rubbish is a serious problem). These include the manmade 400-hectare (1,000-acre) **Lulu Island**, reclaimed back in the 1980s and the much smaller **Horseshoe Island** (Massnou'a) whose well-protected bay has calm waters perfect for easy windsurfing and sailing. The neighbouring island of **Al-Bahrani** is another popular weekend destination for those with access to a boat.

SAADIYAT ISLAND

The 27 sq km (10 sq mile) **Saadiyat Island** ⓭ ('Island of Happiness'; www.saadiyat.ae) is the centrepiece of Abu Dhabi's move to become the cultural capital of the region and an international art centre. The island's three headline developments, all to be housed in spectacular buildings designed by internationally acclaimed architects, are the **Louvre Abu Dhabi**, designed by Jean Nouvel, the **Guggenheim Contemporary Art Museum**, designed by Frank Gehry, and the **Sheikh Zayed National Museum**, designed by Foster and Partners, celebrating the life and times of the UAE's great leader. All three are due to open in 2017 now, although it is common to see projects of this scale get pushed back – sometimes by several years (the original opening date was already 2012). Plans for a **Maritime**

Museum by Tadao Ando and a **Performing Arts Centre** designed by Zaha Hadid have been shelved.

The island is crossed by a single highway, connected by bridge to Al-Mina district in downtown Abu Dhabi on the west, or to neighbouring Yas Island on the east. At the western end of the island, the modest **Manarat al Saadiyat** exhibition (tel: 02-657 5800; www.saadiyatculturaldistrict.ae; daily 9am–10pm) has exhibits on the proposed developments. Close by stands the striking dune-shaped **UAE Pavillion**, designed by Foster & Partners for the Expo 2010 in Shanghai, and subsequently re-erected here. Beyond, the upmarket St Regis and Park Hyatt hotels have already opened, as has the posey Monte Carlo Beach Club and Gary Player-designed Saadiyat Beach Golf Club – although much of the island remains something of a sandy wilderness, with Hawksbill sea turtles still sometimes sighted nesting on the island's public beach.

NORTHERN AND EASTERN ISLANDS

Pending completion of the various mega-projects on Saadiyat, most tourist interest is currently focussed on the gleaming **Yas Island** ⓮ (www.yasisland.ae), named the world's leading tourism project at the 2009 World Travel Awards. The man-made island is accessible from the mainland near the international airport, and also directly from Saadiyat Island. Motorsports are the main draw here, centred on the Yas Marina Circuit, home since 2009 of the Abu Dhabi F1 Grand Prix and squeezed between the island's swanky marina and the spectacular Yas Viceroy Hotel, instantly recognizable thanks to its remarkable glass-and-steel canopy roof, studded with over five thousand LEDs, which twinkle magically after dark.

There are more fast cars and other adrenaline-fuelled action close by at the vast **Ferrari World** theme park (tel:

02-496 8000; www.ferrariworldabudhabi.com; daily 11am–8pm), claimed to be the world's largest indoor theme park, set in a huge building looking something like a huge, bright-red octopus. Attractions range from a white-knuckle rollercoaster and other heart-pumping rides through to gentler attractions and displays on Ferrari's illustrious motor-racing history.

Other attractions scattered about the island include the state-of-the-art **Yas Waterworld** waterpark (www.yaswaterworld.com) and the Kyle Phillips-designed Yas Links golf course (www.yaslinks.com).

OTHER ISLANDS

Just south of Yas is the natural **Al-Samaliyah Island**, for many years a youth adventure centre under the control of the Emirates Heritage Club, with facilities for various activities and traditional sailing vessels.

Taking an abra

Al-Maqtaa Fort

South of Al-Samaliyah is **Sas al-Nakhl Island**, site of the famous **Umm al-Nar archaeological site**, which has given its name to the so-called 'Umm al Nar' period of Arabian Bronze Age prehistory. The island was probably home to a port from where copper was exported from the Al Ain region across the Gulf to the Mesopotamian civilisations 4,000 years ago. As many as 50 communal tombs have been uncovered here, and even though all had been robbed in antiquity, many beautiful items, such as jewellery, necklaces and a gold hairpin, that were found here are now on display in the National Museum at Al Ain (see page 52). Umm al-Nar is currently a high-security oil facility, out of bounds to visitors.

MAINLAND AROUND ABU DHABI CITY

Abu Dhabi City continues to expand onto the mainland and out towards the airport. Several places of interest lie within a short car journey, most just off the main roads out of the city.

BETWEEN THE BRIDGES

Between the Bridges – or Bain al-Jessrain in Arabic – is the name given to a developed area along the waterway separating Abu Dhabi Island and the mainland. The Souk **Qaryat al-Beri** and adjacent hotels now form a lively leisure and nightlife hub, boasting good beaches, bars and restaurants. Shops are laid out in 'Arabian souk' style, with establishments linked by a meandering canal and *abra* water taxis, all with magnificent views across to the Grand Mosque.

Overlooking the water beside the Al-Maqtaa Bridge is **Al-Maqtaa Fort** ⓯, a small building, now completely renovated, which once housed a tourist information office (it is now abandoned). In the middle of the narrow straits below the bridge is an iconic **watchtower**, where even as late as the 1960s soldiers guarded the island against raiders crossing the causeway. Beware of taking photographs in this area, as the bridges are in what is considered a militarily significant area and there is a police station nearby.

EAST TOWARDS THE AIRPORT

East of the Between the Bridges area, on the way to the international airport, is the **Abu Dhabi Golf Club** (see page 86). Being on the mainland, there was plenty of space when this 27-hole course was laid out in the late 1990s. The contrast of

FALCONRY

Abu Dhabi's love of falconry is much more than just a nostalgic memory. For more than 2,000 years, Bedouin tribesmen have used falcons to provide fresh meat in the desert. The birds are used to hunt hares, small gazelles and birds, such as the Houbara Bustard. The two most popular species of falcon are the swift and bold Peregrine falcon (locally known as *shahin*) and the keen-sighted Saker falcon *(hurr)*.

With so much modernisation in Abu Dhabi today, the art of falconry provides a direct link with the simple desert lifestyles of yesteryear. For vivid descriptions of a real Houbara hunt with falcons, read the chapter of *Arabian Sands* when Wilfred Thesiger joins Sheikh Zayed on a month-long 'hawking' expedition in 1948.

Falcons are an important part of Bedouin culture

the green rolling fairways and surrounding barren desert shows what is achievable with modern water-irrigation systems. The lakes and water hazards are wonderfully attractive oases for both native and visiting bird life.

South of here is the great white curving roof and towering floodlights of the **Sheikh Zayed Cricket Stadium**. In just a few years Abu Dhabi has become a major cricket centre, hosting various international twenty20, one-day and test match fixtures. Check local listings for fixtures, which are great events for expat cricket-lovers, many of them from the Indian subcontinent.

FALCON HOSPITAL

Passing the international airport on the left and the nearby Al-Ghazal Sand Golf Club, the E33 road heads out towards Sweihan. Eight kilometres (5 miles) beyond the airport access road, turn right off the E33 just before a slip road signposted 'Bani Yas Graveyard'. Turn immediately right again down a dirt track to the **Abu Dhabi Falcon Hospital** ⓰ (tel: 02-575 5155; www.falconhospital.com; tours Sun–Thur 10am–2pm). Over the last decade this has become a leading centre in Arabia for the analysis and treatment of injured or diseased falcons and other hunting birds, using modern medical facilities while also maintaining links back to the traditions of Emirati desert lifestyle. Visits to the hospital are on two-hour guided tours, all of which must be booked in advance.

Next door is the **Saluki Hunting Dog Centre** (tel: 971 50 658 6669; Sun–Thurs 9am–2pm), where visits must also be organised in advance.

MASDAR

Just a few miles from the airport lies the novel **Masdar** development (www.masdarcity.ae), forming the nucleus of what is eventually intended to become the world's-first zero-carbon city, entirely car-free and using only solar power and other renewable energy resources – an unusual departure for a city built on oil revenues and full of petrol-guzzling vehicles. Scheduled for completion in 2025, the 'city' is planned to provide a home for around 50,000 residents at a cost of US$20 billion. The small section that has been built (to designs by Fosters & Partners) is well worth a visit, full of wacky futuristic architecture. There is a huge postmodern wind-tower and plenty of shady pedestrianized walkways designed to keep out the fierce desert sun and channel any available breezes into the complex, which remains surprisingly cool and pleasant even in the heat of the day.

NORTH TOWARDS DUBAI

Also near the airport on the north coast is the large **Al-Raha Beach Hotel**, which is at the centre of a massive project to develop this whole coastline into a new beachfront city. At present, at area's most striking landmark is the spectacular Aldar HQ building, which you will see driving down the coastal highway to Dubai. Described as 'the world's first circular skyscraper', this is perhaps one of the most remarkable designs anywhere in the region, looking a bit like an enormous magnifying glass held up by a diagonal grid of steel supports.

The verdant Al Raha Beach Hotel

Heading north, the road that runs along the coast joins the main coastal highway to Dubai (E11) at Al-Bahya. On the left here is the **Emirates Park Zoo** (tel: 02-5010000; www.emiratesparkzoo.com; Sun–Wed 9am–8pm, Thur-Sat and public holidays 9am–9pm), where children can learn about and interact with animals such as camels, horses, llamas and kangaroos.

Further along the E11 a road turns off right towards Ajban. The **Dhabian Equestrian Club** is at the Al-Awadi Stables on this road. It is an ideal, quiet location for learning to ride horses and an excellent base for desert rides (see page 89).

AL-WATHBA

The third major highway leaving Abu Dhabi Island is the busy E22 highway to Al Ain, passing over the Al-Mussafah Bridge. Past the junction with the E11 coastal highway and the sprawl of Al-Mafraq and Bani Yas suburbs are a couple of places of interest. On the right is the **Al-Wathba camel-racing track**, where there is great local sporting entertainment in the winter months. Dotted throughout this area are small bushes called white saxaul trees *(Haloxylon persicum)*, also known as 'dew forest', unique to Abu Dhabi. The moisture of inland mists settles on the bushes and drips onto the surrounding ground, sustaining both the plant itself and local wildlife such as hares, foxes, gerbils and various birds.

Nearby is the **Al-Wathba Wetland Reserve** (opened Thur and Sun 8am–1pm, created by accident in 1982 when a leak from a waste-water treatment plant formed nutrient-rich ponds that attracted birds to the area, particularly flamingos. In 2013 it was formally recognized under the Ramsar Convention as a wetland of international significance, with more than 250 species of birds – including huge flocks of flamingos – 11 species of mammals and 10 types of reptiles, including the endangered spiny-tailed lizard, having been identified here. The main seasons for migratory birds are spring and autumn.

NABATI POETRY

With little written history, poetry recitals are the main way for Bedouin traditions to pass through the generations in Arabia. This rhythmic *Nabati* poetry was central to a desert lifestyle that is now a distant memory for most of the population. But as Abu Dhabi moves rapidly ahead, there is an enthusiasm for anything that connects directly with the past.

Nabati recitals are now so popular that a TV talent show called *Million's Poet* is a huge success – a kind of traditional Arabian equivalent to *American Idol* or *X Factor*, with a top prize of over a million dollars. Contestants from around the Arab world read their own compositions in front of the cameras at the 2,000-seat Beach Theatre at the Al-Raha Beach Resort. Some of the poems are delivered almost rap-style, and viewers vote for their favourites.

The largest Dodge pick-up ever made, National Auto Museum

NATIONAL AUTO MUSEUM

Another attraction is located around 40km (25 miles) south of the city, reached by driving west along the E11 then turning off south onto the E65. After driving 14km (9 miles) through the At-Taff region of rugged *sabkha* plains and dry riverbeds, a huge oversized Land Rover on the left announces your arrival at the **National Auto Museum** 17 (tel: 055 749 2155; www.enam.ae; usually open daily 10am–6pm, ring in advance to confirm times and entrance charge). Housed inside a giant purpose-built pyramid, the museum houses the 200-odd vehicles so far collected by 'Rainbow' Sheikh Hamad bin Hamdan Al-Nahyan.

Dominating the whole place is the largest Dodge pick-up ever made, eight times normal size, with five bedrooms inside, accessed by a staircase from the ground. Rows of iconic cars are neatly laid out – US Highway Patrol car, Bedford Army Truck, bubble cars, Pontiac Trans-Ams and Rolls-Royces. Being the Rainbow Sheikh, there are several cars painted in rainbow stripes and even a whole fleet of identical

Mercedes, each in a different rainbow colour – the violet one is particularly stomach-churning. There are plenty of cars to recognise – great 1950s US classics, gull-wings, special Land Rover conversions, military vehicles, futuristic buggies and aeroplane-shaped cars.

Outside, the car park is home to some of the strangest 'vehicles' that you will ever see. A giant earth globe on wheels has bedrooms inside, and nearby is the largest caravan in the world, looking like a beached Mississippi steamboat. Around the back is a Lockheed Tri-Star jumbo jet, which had to be towed in from the nearest landing strip.

AL AIN

The main E22 is a fast motorway that becomes a drag strip of high-speed cars at the end of each day, especially Wednesday and Thursday evenings. Thankfully, trucks use a parallel road, but great care should still be taken. The highway irrigation system has been so successful that most of the desert views are lost to the dense trees and undergrowth, except where the highway swings around a series of curves, amid high sand dunes at Al-Salimat, near to Al Ain International Airport. The highway then comes close to the camel-racing track before easing itself into Al Ain with a view of lofty Jebel Hafeet on the right, if it is not too hazy.

Al Ain is a historical desert town where many city-dwelling locals maintain weekend homes. Nestled beneath Jebel Hafeet and the Hajar Mountains, the 'Oasis City' has an easy-going atmosphere, belying the fact that it is the fourth-largest city in the UAE. Natural springs have always made this area attractive for human habitation, with evidence of settlements 5,000 years ago and as a crucial stopping point for camel caravans crossing the desert. For most of its history, the area was known as Buraimi Oasis, with Al Ain (meaning 'The Spring') just one of the nine separate villages dotted around the area. The others are Hili, Jimi, Qatara, Jahili, Mutaradh and three nowadays in Oman (including Buraimi itself). Not until 2006 were formal UAE/Oman border posts established along the Al Ain/Buraimi boundary.

The heart of each former village is a quiet oasis of lush palm trees, with only the trickling of water along the *falaj* water channels and birdsong to break the silence. All of the old oases still retain a certain degree of autonomy with their own shopping centres, entertainment areas and private forts, but they are increasingly coming within the expanding conurbation of Al Ain. Some of the oldest historical sites are at Hili, with later forts dotted about the different villages.

The Eastern Fort at Al Ain

AROUND AL AIN OASIS

Just a few minutes from the city centre and set within the compound of the Eastern Fort is the **National Museum** ⓲ (Sat–Thur 8.30am–7.30pm, Fri 3–7.30pm, closed Mon). It was established by Sheikh Zayed, who said, 'Those who do not know and appreciate their past will never fully understand where they stand today.' On the left are the rooms dedicated to the archaeological sites, while more modern traditions and culture are explained on the right. Some of the most delicate exhibits are from the ancient tombs and burial sites near Al Ain, including jewellery and a gorgeous red carnelian bracelet from Hili.

There are also important objects such as arrowheads, flints, dagger blades and pottery from the circular tombs at Umm al-Nar and Bida Bint Saud. Some of the most famous objects to be seen here are the finely worked gold and silver animals from the Wadi Suq period (2000–1250BC). A series of life-size figures show the traditions and clothing of the people who have inhabited these oases. Weapons, farm tools, household items, coins, daggers, weaving looms and pearl-diving equipment show what life was like before the oil boom. The natural history section has stuffed birds and falconry equipment.

A traditional silver scabbard at the National Museum

Just outside is the **Eastern Fort** (same opening times as museum), also known as the Sultan Fort, built a century ago during the times of Sheikh Sultan, son of Zayed the First and father of Sheikh Zayed. Some cannons are plinthed at the entrance, and the fort has three round towers for defence. Inside are some restored rooms containing photographs showing the lifestyles of local people over the past 100 years.

Turning left immediately outside of the museum and fort compound takes you through a gateway and into the **Al Ain Oasis** ⓳ (sunrise–sunset; free). Despite its location at the heart of the city, the twisting roads through the palm plantations quickly transport you into a quiet and tranquil setting.

Majlis room in the Al Ain Palace Museum

Only visiting tourists and plantation owners are allowed to drive around the extensive shady plantations; other cars are banned. It is a wonderful area to walk around, and there are signs to the café and mosques within. There are also many birds, attracted not only by the thousands of palm trees, but also by banana, mango and fig trees, and of course the water flowing along the countless constructed channels.

Signposts indicate the way to the 'Sheikh Zayed Old Palace', meaning the **Al Ain Palace Museum** (Sat, Sun & Tues–Thur 8.30am–7.30pm, Fri 3–7.30pm, closed Mon), situated at the western end of the oasis. The museum is a celebration of the life of the father of modern Abu Dhabi. Built in 1937, this series of buildings was Sheikh Zayed's residence in Al Ain when he was appointed as Sheikh Shakhbut's representative.

The open layout of the simple buildings and courtyards encourages even the slightest breeze to cool the rooms. The *majlis* room was used for greeting guests, coffee rooms for hospitality, and there are also kitchens and family rooms. Upstairs is the simple bedroom for the Sheikh and his wife. In one section are paintings of the royal family and an interesting family tree showing the lineage of the Al-Nahyans. The crenelated circular towers either side of the impressive gateway are later additions, inspired by the tiered tower at Jahili Fort.

OTHER SIGHTS IN CENTRAL AL AIN

Jahili Fort ⓴ (Sat, Sun & Tues–Thur 9am–5pm, Fri 3–5pm, closed Mon; free) is situated west of the Al Ain Palace Museum beside one of the *wadis* running through Al Ain. One of the largest forts in the UAE, it is actually two forts in one, with the smaller original version now tucked into the corner of the extensive enclosure. The old fort was started by Sheikh Zayed the First in 1891 and used primarily as a summer residence for the ruling family to escape the heat of the coast. Sheikh Zayed bin Sultan Al-Nahyan was born here sometime around 1918. The nearby circular watchtower dates from the same time and is possibly based on the design of 5,000-year-old fortifications from Hili. The later outer wall linked the fort with the tower and created a large encampment for the Trucial Oman Levies when the soldiers were based here in the 1950s.

Modern alterations have added the visitor information centre, café, bookshop and offices for the Abu Dhabi Authority for Culture and Heritage (http://tcaabudhabi.ae). A series of rooms

Guarding the Al Ain Palace Museum

house a permanent exhibition entitled **Mubarak bin London** – the local name given to explorer Wilfred Thesiger, who journeyed by camel to visit Sheikh Zayed several times in the late 1940s.

Located north of the Eastern Fort, right in the centre of modern Al Ain, is **Al-Murabba Fort** (8am–6pm; free). This steeply tiered square fort was built on the orders of Sheikh Zayed in 1948, just after he became the ruler's representative here. It was originally used as the headquarters of the royal guards, but has also been a civic centre, police station and prison. There are great views from the roof across the modern city to the Eastern Fort.

A ten-minute walk west of the Fort, the **Sheikha Salama Mosque** is the latest addition to Al Ain's urban landscape and the largest mosque in the city, built in a striking postmodern design and with space for five thousands worshippers.

The crenellated battlements of Jahili Fort

The main road (Zayed bin Sultan Street) runs south from here past the Hilton roundabout to the massive **Al-Bawadi Shopping Mall** (www.bawadimall.com).

Al-Muwaiji Fort

The British adventurer Wilfred Thesiger (see page 71) first met Sheikh Zayed after the first of his two historic crossings of the Empty Quarter. Thesiger described Zayed in his classic account of desert exploration, *Arabian Sands*: 'a powerfully built man... his manner was quiet but masterful'. The two men subsequently became very close friends.

AL-JIMI AND AL-QATTARA OASES

North of the centre is the largest single area of palm plantation in the city, split by an access road into Al-Jimi Oasis and Al-Qatara Oasis.

Al-Jimi is still an agricultural centre of working farms and plantations with some old mud houses, mainly belonging to the long established Al-Dhaheri family. The large circular watchtower, known as **Sheikh Ahmad bin Hilal Al-Dhaheri Tower**, defended the local families and their water supply.

Further north, **Al Qattara**'s striking mudbrick fort, topped with sawtooth battlements, has been restored and reopened as the **Al Qattara Arts Centre** (daily except Fri 9am–1pm & 4–8pm; free) hosting exhibitions and workshop space. Several important archaeological sites lie close by, including the 14m (45ft) long Wadi Suq-period **tomb**, where many of the gold ornaments and jewellery now in the National Museum were found. In the oasis are several old mud houses and mosques, plus a mist-cooled restaurant and café. As in all of Al Ain's oases, the water used for irrigation was carried by *falaj* running underground for many kilometres from the Oman Mountains.

Across the road to the west of Al Qattara Oasis is **Al-Murayjib Fort and Park** (8am–6pm; free). This is one of the oldest forts, dating from about 1816 and built as the residence of Sheikh

A versatile tree

The palm tree is highly prized. The trunk is used to build houses, the fronds are woven into mats, bags and furniture, and strands of the leaf are used to make rope. Over 100 varieties of date grow on Abu Dhabi's palm trees, and even the stones can be ground up to make animal fodder.

Shakhbut bin Dhiab. The main building is a large square tower, with a round watch-tower nearby, all within a neat little park.

HILI

North of Al Qattara, **Hili** is the site of the largest Bronze Age settlement in the UAE. Five thousand years ago this was an important area for mining and smelting copper, which was traded with the Mesopotamian civilisations at the other end of the Arabian Gulf. Some of the excavated sites can now be visited as they form part of the **Hili Archaeological Park** ㉑ (Sat–Thur 4.30am–9.30pm, Fri 10am–10pm; free).

Just inside the entrance is a large excavated circular building known as **Hili 10**, made from mud brick and containing a central well. Two similar buildings are nearby, the more striking of which is the reconstructed 4,000-year-old **Grand Tomb**, a communal burial site where hundreds of bodies were interred in the four chambers. Two small entrances allow access into the 12m (40ft) diameter structure, each decorated on the outside with delicate human and animal carvings. The tapering walls would have originally continued to form a dome over the chamber. Another similar tomb nearby has six internal chambers, but was uncovered without bodies. The pit grave known as Tomb N contained 800 skeletons and was possibly a later communal grave where bodies were placed when the more ornate tombs became full. Many of the beautiful objects excavated in and around the tombs can now be seen at the National Museum.

Nearby are two watchtowers standing on large mounds of earth; the circular one is called **Seebat bin Nahyan**, the square one is known as **Sheikh Zayed Murabba**. Both served to protect the village and its water supply. To the west of the oasis are another two forts. **Hili Fort** beside the oasis is now a restaurant, while across the road is **Rumailah Fort**, a two-storey building surrounded by an outer wall, currently closed.

To the north is **Hili Fun City** (June–Sep Mon–Thur 5–10pm Wed ladies and children only, Fri–Sat and public holidays 4–10pm; Oct–May Mon–Thur 4-10pm, Fri–Sat noon–10pm; children under 5 free), an old-fashioned amusement park reserved for families with children.

Around 11km (7 miles) northwest of Hili is a fenced-off outcrop of rock known as **Qarn Bint Saud**. There are reconstructed Hafeet-period tombs and graves here, similar to those found on Jebel Hafeet, as well as the remains of a 3,000-year-old *falaj* that once carried water from the mountains.

Reconstructed burial tomb at Hili Archaeological Park

AL AIN ZOO

On the southern edge of Al Ain, nestled at the foot of the first ridges of Jebel Hafeet is the excellent **Al Ain Zoo** ㉒ (www.alainzoo.ae; daily 8am–9pm). The zoo has over 4,000 animals, the first enclosure containing hundreds of lively gazelles, watched by more cautious oryx. The park specialises in preserving Arabian species such as tahrs and oryx, but they also have giraffes and hippos, long lost from Arabia. The zoo's breeding programme plays an important role in helping to protect rare indigenous wildlife, with well over 50 antelopes and gazelles born here each year. If you miss a visit to Abu Dhabi's Falcon Hospital, the evening 'Bird of Prey Show' gives you the opportunity to see falcons, owls and eagles up close.

JEBEL HAFEET

One of Abu Dhabi's most striking natural features is the rugged shark-tooth outline of the 1,240m (4,070ft) high **Jebel Hafeet** ㉓, south of Al Ain. This major geological feature was an important landmark for early travellers crossing the desert towards the water of the nearby springs.

Stone-built **tombs** were erected up to 5,000 years ago along the eastern and northern slopes of the mountain. The era in which the graves were created (3200–2700BC) is now known as the Hafeet period. It is thought that up to 10 bodies would have been placed in each circular 'beehive' tomb, and later Bronze and Iron Age items found in them suggest that they were reused many times. A guide and 4x4 vehicle are needed to find the tomb sites.

A tarmac road winds up Jebel Hafeet with plenty of good viewing and parking places on the way. At the top is a huge car park and the cavernous **Top of Hafeet Mountain Café**, which becomes an impromptu gathering place at sunset for spectacular views over the surrounding desert. Just below the summit is the **Mercure Hotel**, also with stunning views, especially from the terrace bar and pool. The whole mountain is popular with rock climbers and trekkers during the cooler months.

At the foot of the mountain on the western side is the open landscaped area of **Green Muzzabarah** (24 hrs; free),

The winding road to Jebel Hafeet

with cafés, horse carriages and kids' rides. These stretches of rolling green countryside at the foot of the lifeless jagged rocks of Jebel Hafeet are an extremely popular spot for family picnics and chilling out at the end of the day, especially at weekends. Further round, there are swimming pools, a large boating lake and hot springs.

THE CAMEL SOUK AND MAZYAD FORT

On the eastern side of Jebel Hafeet is Al-Zahir, an area steeped in the breeding, rearing and training of camels. In the late afternoon, strings of highly prized camels can be seen walking and jogging along the training tracks beside the road. Al Ain's famous **Camel Souk** can also be found here and is a lively sight most mornings, with picturesque dromedaries tied up in pens – although pushy traders may demand outrageous sums of money in return for showing you around or letting you take photos of their animals. The souk is just off the road towards the Oman border at Mazyad. About 6km from

Relaxing on the Green Muzzabarah

the Hilton hotel you will see the huge Bawadi mall on your left. Do a U-turn at the next roundabout, 1km or so beyond the mall, and start driving back towards Al Ain. The souk is off the road on your right, about 500m before you get back to the Bawadi mall.

Further south is Mazyad and the border with Oman. Around 200m/yds before the main road reaches the swooping white tents of the border post, a right turn at a roundabout leads towards a white mosque in the distance. At the large gates, ask for permission to visit the fort and enter the palm plantation. Follow this road for about 1km (0.5 miles) until **Mazyad Fort** ㉔ (sunrise–sunset; free) appears on the left. This is the most atmospheric of all Al Ain's forts due to its remote location at the foot of the looming Jebel Hafeet. Watchtowers at each of the four corners were used to look out for approaching raiders, but now afford great views over the palm trees. On the slopes around the plantation are some reconstructed Hafeet tombs.

NORTH OF AL AIN

North of Hili, the main road towards the neighbouring emirates of Dubai and Sharjah is the E66. The road runs north past the poultry farms of **Al-Heyer** into Dubai Emirate at Al-Faqah, but just before the border is a right turn to **Shwaib** (Shuayb; signposted Fujeirah 141km/87 miles). This pleasant road of undulating orange-coloured sand dunes dotted with clumps of tamarisks and wandering camels enters Sharjah Emirate after 15km (10 miles).

A useful alternative way back to Abu Dhabi City is the E33, which heads west from Al-Heyer through the desert town of **Sweihan** (Suwayhan) before going past the Falcon Hospital on the outskirts of Abu Dhabi City.

LIWA OASIS

Viewed from space, Liwa Oasis is such a dominant feature that it is easy to see why it has had such an influence on the lives of the inhabitants of Abu Dhabi. The thin crescent-shaped strip of greenery curves gracefully for over 100km (60 miles), between thousands of square kilometres of giant sand dunes that seem to threaten to smoother it. This is not a Hollywood-style oasis with a few palm trees dotted around a pool of fresh water, but a mass of vegetation, whose roots tap underground water reserves that originated thousands of years before on the other side of Arabia.

From the earliest times the oasis provided a refuge for humans. Each family or tribe set up a fort to protect its sources of water, food and trade at the oasis. The first members of the Bani Yas

Omani border

The border with Oman runs just south of Mazyad Fort, up one side of Jebel Hafeet and down the other, cutting the mountain in half. The northern half belongs to Abu Dhabi and the southern half to Oman.

Bedouin hospitality

Bedouin hospitality is legendary and has deep social significance. An offer of coffee assures the guest of their safety; a meal or overnight stay signifies greater protection within the tribal territory. If a traveller is harmed while in their care, the host is obliged to avenge it.

tribe probably arrived here in the late 16th century, setting up an alliance with the native Mansuri tribe. Two-and-a-half centuries ago this oasis was the stronghold of Bani Yas tribal territory, a base from which intrepid parties ventured forth to establish the coastal settlements that would become Abu Dhabi and Dubai. Today there is still ample water at the oasis for huge irrigated farms, and the area is now accessible from Abu Dhabi City in just a few hours.

ROUTES TO LIWA

Three main roads, all roughly parallel to each other, link Abu Dhabi's coastal highway E11 with Liwa Oasis. The largest and fastest is the central **E45**, which leaves the E11 some 95km (60 miles) from Abu Dhabi Island and runs through the desert town of Madinat Zayed to meet the oasis at its main administrative centre of Mezaira. Though a public bus runs from Abu Dhabi City to Mezaira, once in Liwa it is not possible to travel around or visit any sites using public transport.

Though the E45 is the fastest route from Abu Dhabi City to the oasis, the easterly **E65** offers the advantage of passing the National Auto Museum (see page 50) on the way. This road leaves the E11 some 35km (22 miles) from Abu Dhabi Island and reaches Liwa Oasis at its most easterly settlement – Hamim. The full length of the road is fenced, primarily to prevent camels wandering into the path of vehicles, while underpasses allow them to graze safely on either side. The only respites from the endless sand dunes of the Ramlat al-Hamrah are the occasional farms and plantations. Some roads branch off this desert road towards the oilfields at Sahil and Asab, but a special permit is required to take them.

The third road is the most westerly, departing the E11 some 200km (125 miles) from Abu Dhabi at Ruwais, and then passing through Ghayathi before eventually reaching Umm Hisin at the western end of Liwa Oasis.

EASTERN LIWA

Arriving at the eastern end of Liwa via the E65, the settlement of **Hamim** suddenly announces itself with lush green fields full of crops. Just west of the village, a 4x4 track turns south-east off the main road through the oasis towards the distant **Umm al-Zumul** region where the UAE, Saudi Arabia and Oman borders all meet. Parts of this remote area have been excavated, uncovering more than 80 Neolithic sites with evidence

Driving through the desert

Liwa Oasis

of human habitation. The climate must have been cooler then, with evidence of lakes, good grazing and hunting some 6–7,000 years ago. One of the sites is at **Yaw Sahhab**, only 9km (5.5 miles) from Hamim. The luxurious Qasr al Sarab Desert Resort (see page 140) is located in the same area.

The steeply undulating road that runs through the oasis, connecting small desert farms every few kilometres, was only constructed in the 1980s. Halfway to the main oasis town of Mezaira is the settlement of **Jarrah**, a local centre for camel breeding. On the right, set behind Jabbanah Market is **Jabbanah Fort** (8am–sunset; free), whose three towers can be seen above the palm trees. If the gateway is locked, go around the back and enquire at the nearby house. Experts from Al Ain restored the fort in 2004 and there are wonderful views from the upper floor over the fields, plantations and orchards.

The next major settlement is **Shah**, after which is a signpost reading 'Mezaira 11km'. Take the next right turn towards Mahdhar Attab and after 500m/yds an access road to the right leads to **Al-Meel Fort** (8am–sunset; free), known locally as Qasr Attab. Surrounded by lush plantations, this is another impressive three-tower fort that gives great views north up another major *wadi*. The fort is strategically placed at the meeting of these two major routes and is thought to have been constructed in 1816–18, during the reign of Sheikh Mohammed bin Shakhbut bin Dhiab. Continuing east, a series of decorated roundabouts signal the arrival into Mezaira Town.

MEZAIRA TOWN

Mezaira is the main administrative and shopping centre of Liwa Oasis, from where the main E12 road heads north to Madinat Zayed and the coast. Continuing westwards from the centre of Mezaira Town, the road drops down and the majestic **Liwa Hotel** can be seen at the end of an access road to the left.

On the other side of the main road are the towers of another fort, reached by a short tarmac road. This is **Mezaira Fort** ㉕ (8am–sunset; free), a series of empty rooms with beautiful carved wooden doors. Notice the practical use of palm trees – trunks for roof support, frond covering for the ceilings and hollowed-out palm trunks for guttering to send rainwater away from the vulnerable mud-covered walls. Wooden steps lead to the top of all three towers.

A few kilometres further along is a large mud house set beside the main road on the right. This is the **Al-Hamily Tribe House** (8am–sunset; free), also known as Dhafeer

THE FORTS OF LIWA

In such an inhospitable place, the series of forts running along the Liwa Oasis indicate how protective the tribes were of their cultivable land and scarce resources. The main purpose of the forts was as watchtowers, controlling the major routes in and out of the oasis, as it was common for other tribes to send well-armed forces on raids to steal camels. A square fort would normally have a tower in each corner, but in Liwa there are usually three towers, one either side of the front entrance and just a single one to cover the rear. All are based upon similar designs, but each is slightly different. Inside the towers, wooden ladders or steep staircases can be used to access the roof, but beware the poor quality of the ladders and the very small access holes at the top.

The three distinctive towers of Mezaira Fort

Fort, consisting of a single two-storey tower house, giving a great idea of how large tribal families used to live. The defensive style can be compared to a small military fort of a single defendable tower within its own walled area. Stairs give access to the roof with more great views across the plantations, fields and dunes. The next roundabout is just beyond the Police Station, with the road to Moreeb Dunes going left.

MOREEB DUNES

One of the main reasons tourists come to Liwa is to drive 30km (18 miles) out to the **Moreeb Dunes** ㉖ and access the surrounding desert using 4x4 vehicles. The tarmac road to Moreeb goes south from the Police Station roundabout, past the old Liwa Rest House and the Industrial Zone. Some loose sand blows across the tarmac, but it is quite safe for non-4x4 vehicles to reach Moreeb. The final destination is a flat area completely surrounded by sand dunes.

Tal Moreeb (meaning 'Scary Hill') is the highest dune at over 200m (660ft) and the steepest at 50 percent (1 in 1). In January/February, grandstands are erected around the dune for the Moreeb Hill Races, as drivers race their noisy 4x4s and motorbikes up the steep shifting slopes to the top of the dune, while camel races and saluki hunting dog trials are also held. At any time of the year it is an invigorating drive to watch the sunset anywhere among these giant dunes. The large black birds seen constantly patrolling the dunes are usually Brown-necked ravens (*Corvus rufficolis*).

WESTERN LIWA

At the same roundabout near the Police Station, the road north goes towards **Mariah al-Sharqiya** (Eastern al-Mariah), while the main road is signposted Aradah and continues west up a hill and past the boy's school on the right. On the other side of the hill, look out for a single tower behind palm trees on the right and take the tarmac access road before the top of the next hill. This is the small **Qutuf Fort** (8am–sunset; free), beautifully situated in front of a sand dune, surrounded by palm groves. Much simpler than the other forts, there are just a couple of rooms and a staircase leading to a single tower, now full of pigeons. Beside it is a small white mosque with a tiny minaret, visited by Wilfred Thesiger in 1948.

Further along the main road, beyond a series of large green fields on the right at Radoum is a petrol station and a right turning

Saluki dogs

Desert Bedouin have used saluki hunting dogs for thousands of years to hunt small animals and birds. Known for their speed over short distances, they provided fresh meat to supplement the Bedouin diet of camel's milk and dates. As with camels and falcons, the best breeds are highly prized today.

Camping in the desert

to **Khannur**. This is said to have been the first capital of Liwa Oasis during the reign of Sheikh Shakhbut bin Dhiab. The Bani Yas tribe constructed one of their first forts here in 1793, but it was later destroyed.

To reach Mariah al-Gharbiya (Western al-Mariah) and Al-Hayla Tower, take this right turn towards Khannur. For **Mariah al-Gharbiya** turn left at the next roundabout, go straight across the next roundabout and after 1km (0.6 miles) take the left fork signposted Al-Id. A single tower can be seen on the right side, known as **Mariah al-Gharbiya Fort**. For **Al-Hayla Fort**, turn right at the first roundabout. The fort (in a poor state of preservation) is in the middle of a palm plantation about 300m/yds away.

Towards the western end of the main road is Liwa's final historic fort, the easily missed **Umm Hisin** (8am–sunset; free). Also referred to as Aradah Fort, it is on the right-hand side just before the final roundabout from where the western access road goes to Ghayathi and the coast. The ruins are about 700m/yds away and are said to be the site of the last battle ever fought in the emirate, when in the late 1880s defenders from Liwa held off an attack by raiders from Qatar. Access is through a plantation and then across open rough ground requiring four-wheel drive. This (along with Al-Hayla Fort) is one of the very few forts in the UAE not yet restored. The protective fence is there to stop building contractors from stealing the few remaining stone blocks of what must have once been an impressive circular stone building, thought to be around 200 years old.

The roundabout with the road to Ghayathi signals the western end of the oasis, but the modern tarmac road continues for a further 20km (12 miles) to a police and military base near the Saudi Arabian border. The road makes this part of the **Empty Quarter Desert** accessible for 4x4 adventures, but unlike the unspoilt Moreeb Dunes area, there are giant electricity pylons marching across the desert and limitations as to how close you can get to the Saudi border without causing suspicion.

AL-GHARBIA

Over 70 percent of the landmass of the entire UAE is designated as Al-Gharbia – the Western Region. The vast expanses of the region are primarily the domain of oil workers and engineers, with several major oilfields in the region. Until the

WILFRED THESIGER

The British explorer Wilfred Thesiger made two crossings of the Empty Quarter Desert in the late 1940s with camels and help from Rashid Bedouin tribesmen. His great desert adventures are recounted in his epic book *Arabian Sands*, published in 1959.

In 1947 the group came close to Liwa, but Thesiger remained in the desert just to the south. His companions tried to buy food at the oasis, but returned with just a few poor-quality dates. On the second crossing they left Wadi Hadramaut in southern Yemen in January 1948 and arrived at Liwa Oasis eight weeks later. In his descriptions of Liwa, Thesiger mentions passing through the settlements of Qutuf and Dhafeer, before taking another week to ride on to Abu Dhabi Island. Thesiger returned to Liwa for a more leisurely look around later that year, after staying with Sheikh Zayed at Al Ain (see page 55).

mid-1970s the border stretched to meet Qatar at the Khor al-Udaid inlet, but resolving the Buraimi problem in the east meant losing 60km (37 miles) of coastline to the Saudis in the west. Plans to exploit Al-Gharbia's tourist potential are still in their early stages, and for the time being relatively few visitors come out this way.

ANCIENT LAND

The western border with Saudi Arabia now runs along the **Sabkhat Matti**, an area of treacherous salt flats that was one of the most dangerous sections of Wilfred Thesiger's journey to Liwa in 1948. But the crusty mud also holds some secrets that are only now being revealed. Water seeping to the surface from underground aquifers created marshy areas that recorded the movements of animals over millions of years, including extinct sabre-toothed cats, four-tusked elephants

Flamingos on the deserted coast of Al-Gharbia

and giant ostrich. Fossil footprints of ancient elephants are laid out across the mudflats at Mleisa near Ghayathi, on the westerly road to Liwa Oasis. An almost complete Late Miocene fossil elephant skeleton was discovered near Ruwais, and other important finds of apes, hippos and antelopes uncovered between Tarif and Jebel Dhanna.

This entire coastline must at one time have been lush savannah for such large mammals to thrive here about 7 million years ago. Ongoing research in the area could provide important links showing how the differences between African and Asian animals evolved. Evidence of human occupation as long as 150,000 years ago has also been found at Jebel Barakah. These fossil sites are well protected and currently not open to the public.

MADINAT ZAYED

The main settlement on the road running between Mezaira and the coast is **Madinat Zayed**, currently being developed as a weekend resort area to attract visitors from the crowded cities of Abu Dhabi and Dubai. One plan is to create vast areas of forest around Madinat Zayed that can sustain large numbers of native animals such as oryx, which will be reintroduced. The Al-Dhafra Camel Festival takes place here each December, complete with a beauty pageant for camels.

To the east of Madinat Zayed is a large fort known as **Mantiqa al-Sirra**, possibly an early fortification around a well or date plantation and important enough at one time to be defended by cannons. Pottery dating from the 16th or 17th century has been found, suggesting that it could be the site of Ezh-Zhafrah fort, mentioned in Omani history, which played an important role in Omani–Bani Yas tribal relationships as far back as 1633. Some of the roads in this area are only for use by authorised oil and gas personnel, and you will be turned back at the checkpoints unless you have the correct permits.

THE WESTERN COAST

The major E11 highway runs the entire length of coastline from Dubai in the northeast to the Saudi border in the west. Care must be taken when driving as it is usually full of painfully slow trucks and speeding cars – often a lethal combination. The road is mostly a few kilometres inland with the occasional track leading to wonderfully serene coastal lagoons, full of wading birds such as greater flamingos, curlews and sand plovers.

The port of **Tarif** is mentioned a lot on signposts, but is mainly a base for oil and gas support companies. The coastal town of **Mirfa** ㉗, on the other hand, is a pleasant, laid-back resort with several cafés and good watersports, especially kite-surfing and windsurfing due to the permanent strong winds, including an annual festival (www.algharbiafestivals.com/watersports). Approaching the town, eroded columns standing several metres above the salt flats indicate where the seabed used to be when the sea level here was a lot higher.

Mirfa is a kite-surfer's playground

The coast around here is all part of the huge **Marawah Marine Protected Area** (MMPA), named after the nearby island. This is the largest marine protection area in the Arabian Gulf and the first Unesco Biosphere Reserve in the UAE, containing mangroves, sea grasses, coral reefs, dolphins, turtles and the world's densest population of dugongs (sea cows). **Marawah Island** itself is an important historical site with evidence of continual human occupation since the Stone Age, including the oldest human skeleton found so far in the UAE. Two beautiful pearl oyster shell buttons found in the tomb indicate that pearl-diving was already taking place 7,500 years ago. The foundations of a 6th-century **Nestorian Monastery** similar to the one on Sir Bani Yas (see page 79) have also been uncovered. Anyone wishing to visit the MMPA should apply for a permit from the Environment Agency (tel: 02-445 4777; email: customerservice@ead.ae; www.ead.ae).

Jacques Cousteau

In the mid-1950s, the world-famous underwater explorer Jacques-Yves Cousteau was employed to use his newly invented scuba gear to search for oil. His seabed survey off Das Island helped to identify an anticline – a geological feature that often holds oil reserves – and in this case, rather a lot of it.

Further west is the headland of **Jebel Dhanna** ㉘, site of another couple of beach resorts, both run by Danat Hotels and popular weekend destinations for the workers in the area. The larger Danat Resort Jebel Dhanna has a wonderful private stretch of white sand and offers snorkelling and deep-sea fishing excursions. The Dhafra Beach hotel is close by, next to the **Al-Dhafra Golf Links**, which advertises itself as 'probably the cheapest golf club in the world'. There are no shops or restaurants here, but plenty back on the main coast road at **Ruwais**, which services the oil industry.

A great number of islands lie off the western coast, many with evidence of human occupation from a range of periods, but most are privately owned, protected or have restricted access. For the time being only two islands are easily

The luxurious resort on Sir Bani Yas Island

accessible, Sir Bani Yas and Dalma, both reached from Jebel Dhanna. Sir Bani Yas is the first of a cluster of eight islands that are intended to eventually open to tourism under the collective 'Desert Islands' moniker, with the emphasis on very upmarket eco-tourism – see www.desertislands.com for more information.

SIR BANI YAS ISLAND

Sir Bani Yas Island ㉙ is a highlight of any trip to Abu Dhabi – a perfect mix of laid-back luxury and adventure. Around half the island is protected as the Arabian Wildlife Park, a nature reserve for indigenous flora and fauna originally established by Sheikh Zayed in 1971. The foundation of the project was the planting of 2.5 million trees, which has turned a dusty salt island into a lush savannah-like environment capable of sustaining large numbers of animals.

Boat transfers from Jebel Dhanna are privately operated from the Desert Islands visitor centre at the end of a long sand spit to the north of the harbour. Cars are left in the car park. There are also charter flights from Abu Dhabi City (a 25-minute journey). There are currently two ways to visit the island: the most memorable (and expensive) option is to stay overnight on the island; a more affordable alternative is to take the three-hour island tour from the Danat Resort Jebel Dhanna in Jebel Dhanna. Options of places to stay on the island include the lavish Desert Islands Resort and Spa (see page 141), overlooking a lagoon at the northern end of the island, and the Anantara Al Sahel Villas and Anantara Al Yamm Villas (www.anantara.com).

The experience begins as soon as you arrive at the island's dock or small airstrip – even the transfer to the resort (aboard one of the world's first two zero-emission buses) provides game-viewing opportunities. The resort offers a wide programme of activities including game drives, guided walks, mountain-biking, horse-riding, snorkelling, scuba-diving, kayaking and archery.

Some of the most popular excursions are the **gamedrives** to see the wide variety of animals that have been introduced to the island. Led by knowledgeable rangers in special game-viewing vehicles, most visits are early morning or late afternoon, when the animals are most active. Spread around

SALT DOME ISLANDS

Both Sir Bani Yas and Dalma are salt dome islands, formed between 5 and 10 million years ago. Salt domes are created when the repeated flooding and evaporation of sea water in coastal shallows leaves a large salt deposit, which is then buried under layers of sediment. As the submerged salt warms under pressure it becomes mobile and, being lighter than the rocks above it, pushes its way back up to the surface. As it rises, it often captures a layer of oil and gas on the way. Not all salt domes reach the surface, but the oil and gas they hold can be released by drilling. Where they do reach the surface, pieces of other geological layers are also brought up, making the salt dome islands fascinating places to see and study the earth's geological processes.

Humans have mined salt on Sir Bani Yas for thousands of years, and the remains of six salt mines can be seen in Wadi al-Milh (Salt Valley) on the western slopes of the central mountain. The salt also supplies vital minerals for animals, which use them as 'salt licks'.

the island are herds of reintroduced Arabian oryx, ostrich and gazelle. More exotic animals suited to these conditions include Beisa oryx, eland, Indian spotted deer, blackbuck, urial and reticulated giraffe.

Now that a young cheetah called Safira has been released 'into the wild' to roam the rugged interior of the island, the tame 'safari park' impression has been blown wide open. Surviving on her own instincts, Safira hunts the gazelles and antelopes, and word of a new kill spreads quickly around the resort. The project is still in its infancy, and the plan is to release more animals from the safety of their compounds.

Safira the cheetah makes a kill on Sir Bani Yas Island

Another option is a **game walk** into the interior to see some of the amazing geological features of this unique island – and maybe some wildlife. The trekking can be as hard or easy as you choose, with tremendous views after a tough hike up one of the mountains. Marked trails can be undertaken without guides; one of the best for bird watching is around the resort's lagoon and sand spit.

The release of Safira the cheetah has somewhat restricted the number of **mountain-bike** trails, but there are enough safe off- and on-road routes for interesting and challenging rides, again led by guides. Bikes, helmets and equipment are provided. **Horse-riding** is also available through the Sir Bani Yas Stables, offering a particularly enjoyable way of exploring the island.

There are plenty of options for exploring the waters around Sir Bani Yas too. The island now has its own **watersports** and **dive** centre offering the chance to spot dolphins and even the elusive dugong. The Rock Reef is about 300m/yds offshore, attracting many fish, green turtles and stingrays, while to the north is a shipwreck full of fish off Ghashah Island. Guided **snorkelling** trips allow visitors to explore the island's beautiful reefs and abundant sealife, while **kayaking** trips take visitors into a mangrove area to see the coastal environment, and **deep-sea fishing** trips can also be arranged. To the northeast is Umm Qassar Island, which attracts many birds and **birdwatchers**.

There are also several sites of archaeological interest on Sir Bani Yas, one of the most important being a large **Nestorian monastery and church** in the east of the island. There are remains of stucco decorative crosses, motifs and figures dating from AD600. A great deal of work still has to be done at the site, which is now covered for protection.

Pearl-diving

For hundreds of years world-class pearls (*lulu* in Arabic) came from these shallow waters, where pearling boats sailed for about four months between June and September each year. Weighted down and sustained only by a lung full of air, divers would sink to the seabed and collect the oysters in net baskets.

DALMA ISLAND

At first sight two things strike you about **Dalma Island** ㉚ (www.dalmaisland.com). The first is its strange shape – the circular island has a huge manmade tail running south to the palace of a sheikh. The second is how green it is, thanks to

Al-Meraikhi House on Dalma Island

the ample supply of fresh water from around 200 wells. This excellent water supply brought humans to this 'salt dome' island around 7,000 years ago. Several archaeological sites are being investigated on the island, and the most significant finds include pieces of Ubaid pottery indicating early trade with Mesopotamia at the head of the Gulf. The fertile soil and reliable water supply meant that a century ago it was the only permanently inhabited pearling centre, regularly supplying Abu Dhabi island with water.

The island is 32km (20 miles) offshore, roughly 9km (5.5 miles) in length, and has about 5,000 inhabitants, mainly fishermen and farmers. The main tourist sights are a pearl merchant's house and three nearby mosques, all located in the middle of town. The restored two-storey **Al-Meraikhi Old House** is now home to the small **Dalma Museum** (tel: 02-516 4389; Sat–Thur 8am–4pm; free), which exhibits local finds and gives a good account of the island's pearling and maritime history. Built with coral blocks covered in gypsum plaster in 1931, the name comes from Mohammed bin Jasim Al-Meraikhki (or Al-Muraykhi), who traded pearls from here. The British and Indian currency on display was used during the boom years of pearl-trading a century ago. The rooms, which were windowless for pearl security, also contain interesting sections on Dalma's anthropology.

Al-Yasat Islands

Just before the Saudi border are the Al-Yasat Islands, part of the Al-Yasat Marine Protected Area, helping to protect the coastline and marine life. Permits are required to visit the area, available from the Environment Agency (see page 75).

Surrounding the house are three restored mosques, none of which has a minaret. They all show distinctive local Gulf elements in their construction, such as a protruding *mihrab* in the *qibla* wall and low windows below false arches. The mosques cannot be entered by non-Muslims, but are easy to view from outside. Immediately behind the museum is the **Al-Meraikhi Mosque**, a small solid building with access from the courtyard, decorated in two-tone brown. In the centre of the square, the **Al-Dawsari Mosque** has false corner pillars and an attached ablution building. Access from the courtyard is through a portico held up by carved pillars. The third is the **Al-Muhannadi** (or Al-Mahdi) **Mosque**, more secluded under trees with loudspeakers at the corners of the roof. Similar in design to the others, it also has an ablution room and portico held up with eroded columns.

The public car ferry to Dalma takes 1hr 30min to cross to the island, leaving Jebel Dhanna Sat–Thurs at 6am, 11.15am and 3.45pm, and on Fri at 7am and 3.45pm. Cars can be left in the port car park or taken on the ferry, and passport details have to be registered at the small police office. Ferries return from Dalma at 9am, 1pm and 6pm (Fri at 10am and 6pm).

WHAT TO DO

There is no shortage of things to do in and around Abu Dhabi, from shopping at top-class malls to watching sporting superstars at the Formula 1 Grand Prix. Golf, horse riding and water sports are all popular outdoor activities, while ice-skating and ten-pin bowling are great ways to hide from the heat. Expat workers have created specialist clubs for almost every activity, from triathlons to birdwatching. In the evenings there is a choice of live music and nightclubs, plus the chance to catch a one-off concert or performance.

SPORTS AND OUTDOOR ACTIVITIES

SPECTATOR SPORTS

Football. Football is the nation's most popular sport. Sheikh Mansour bin Zayed Al-Nahyan (a brother of Abu Dhabi ruler Sheikh Khalifa) bought the English team Manchester City in 2008 and is also chairman of local team Al-Jazira, one of four that currently represent Abu Dhabi City in the UAE Football League Premier Division. The emirate's most successful club, however, is Al Ain FC, who won their fourteenth league title in 2013, and who were also Asian Champions in 2003. Matches are played at the main stadiums throughout the winter season, and English teams often visit off-season.

Cricket. The high number of expat workers from the subcontinent has raised interest in cricket over the past 20 years. Near the airport, the Sheikh Zayed Cricket Stadium (www.adcricketclub.ae) is a world-class venue for international one-day and test matches, and has hosted several matches featuring the Pakistan national side since 2009,

The Shangri-La's pool gives great views of the Sheikh Zayed Mosque

Jet skiers in the waters beside Adu Dhabi City's Corniche

following the ban prohibiting them from staging matches in their own country.

Powerboat racing. Abu Dhabi hosts one of the seven-odd races in the annual F1 Powerboat World Championship (www.f1h2o.com) – a bit like a Formula 1 Grand Prix on water, with the course laid out just off the Corniche, giving spectators great opportunities to watch the action. They also boast one of the championships leading teams – Team Abu Dhabi – featuring local drivers Thani al-Qamzi and Mohammed Al-Mehairbi.

***Dhow* racing.** For an altogether more serene and traditional form of boat racing, nothing beats the *dhow* races held regularly off the coast of Abu Dhabi in the winter months. Most of the wooden craft competing have been lovingly restored to the highest standards, while races also offer a rare chance to see these old boats under their distinctive triangular lateen sails – engines now power most *dhows*. Check the website of the Abu Dhabi Sailing and Yacht Club (www.adsyc.ae) for details of forthcoming events.

Camel racing. The sight of camels racing across the desert is one of Abu Dhabi's most memorable sights, with races held at the Al Wathba Camel Race Track (45km east of Abu Dhabi on the way to Al Ain; tel: 02 583 9200) and at the Al Maqam Track close to Al Ain. Races are usually held very early in the morning on Thursdays, Fridays and national holidays during the winter months. Entrance is free.

WATER SPORTS

Every conceivable watersport is available in Abu Dhabi, from windsurfing, kite-surfing and wake-boarding to water-skiing, jet-skiing, sailing and yachting. **Jet skis** can be hired by the hour at some of the beach resorts and are popular off the Corniche towards sunset. Empros Eywoa Watersports (tel: (0) 50 166 9396; www.eywoa.com) organise a wide range of watersports, while wakeboarding and water-skiing is available at the Al Forsan Resort (tel: 02-556 8555; www.alforsan.com. Unusual kayaking trips through the mangrove swamps fringing the city can be organized through the Anantara hotel (tel: 02-656 1000; www.abu-dhabi.anantara.com) and Sea Hawk Watersports (tel: 02-673 6688; www.sea-hawk.ae). The

FORMULA 1 GRAND PRIX

Abu Dhabi's blue ribbon sporting event is unquestionably the annual Formula 1 Grand Prix, held since 2009 at the circuit on Yas Island (www.yasmarinacircuit.ae). The track combines the waterside glitz of Monte Carlo (complete with attached marina) and the stunningly futuristic Yas Viceroy Hotel, built right over the track. Superb race views from the west grandstand become even more action-packed if cars fail to make the tight bend at the end of the long straight, since the run-off area passes right under the seating.

permanently windy conditions at Mirfa make it an ideal location for **windsurfing** and **kite-surfing**, and it is also home to the annual Al-Gharbia watersports festival.

Many beach resort hotels offer guests the chance to **swim** in the warm waters of the Gulf, and there is an excellent, Blue Flag **public beach** right in the centre of the city, towards the western end of the Corniche. In accordance with Islamic traditions, all beach visitors should be modestly dressed.

Diving. Shallow depths and generally poor visibility limit diving off the Abu Dhabi coast, but there are some outcrops of coral with colourful fish, a few small shipwrecks such as the *Jasim* and MV *Ludwig*, plus the chance to see turtles, dolphins and even the elusive dugong. Reliable local operators include Emirates Divers (www.emiratesdivers.com), Al Mahara Diving Centre (www.divemahara.com), Ocean Dive Center (www.oceandivecenter.ae) and Sea Hawk Water Sports (www.seahawk.ae), offering a full range of PADI-certified courses and dives. Courses in freediving (diving without scuba equipment) are offered by Freediving UAE (www.freedivinguae.com).

Sport fishing. Big-game fishing trips offering open-sea adventure and the chance to land sailfish, queenfish and trevally can be arranged through Arabian Divers and Sport Fishing Charters (www.fishabudhabi.com).

OUTDOOR SPORTS AND ACTIVITIES

Golf. With the emirate's huge investment in intricate watering systems, some amazing golf courses have been created in the desert. Designed to professional standards, they often host European Tour events that attract the world's top players during the winter. Several courses (all open to non-members) on and around Abu Dhabi Island offer beautifully manicured fairways and a relaxed atmosphere. Arguably the best of these is Abu Dhabi Golf Club (Sas al-Nakhl; tel: 02-885 3555; www.adgolfclub.

com), a 27-hole 'super course' on the mainland near Abu Dhabi City, run by the prestigious Troon Golf management company. Other courses include Yas Links (Yas Island; tel: 02-810 7710; www.yaslinks.com), a superb 18-hole course (plus floodlit par-3 nine-hole course); the older (and less expensive) Abu Dhabi City Golf Club (Al Mushrif; tel: 02-445 9600; www.adcitygolf.ae), a verdant nine-hole course close to city centre; and the unusual Al Ghazal Golf Club (near the airport; tel: 02-505 5023; www.al ghazalgolf.ae), one of the world's finest sand courses. In Al Ain, the Palm Sports Resort (tel: 03-768 4888; www.aesgclub.com), just off the road to Abu Dhabi, has a good nine-hole course.

Tennis. A number of larger hotels have tennis courts for guests' use, and there are also top-class facilities available at the Abu Dhabi International Tennis Complex (tel: 02-403 4200; www.zsc.ae/en/10/facilities/international-tennis-center) at Zayed Sports City, including six practice courts, plus coaching.

The perfectly manicured course at Abu Dhabi Golf Club

Desert safaris. Day or overnight safaris into the emirate's desert interior give a real taste of the region's harsh environment, most easily arranged through a local tour operator (see page 122). Be aware of the risks involved if you decide to organize your own safari without a professional guide – the desert in the hinterlands of Abu Dhabi emirate can be a large, lonely and potentially dangerous place, and any journey off-road should be well-equipped for and organised. Never head out into the desert with just a single vehicle, and make sure that someone experienced is in charge of navigation, communication and equipment.

Hiking. Some of the terrain here is perfect for adventure walks and treks, especially in the winter months. Ascents of the rugged Jebel Hafeet near Al Ain can be made by several routes. Hikes on Sir Bani Yas Island are arranged through the resort, with a wide choice of both easy and tough hikes

A hike on Sir Bani Yas Island promises some spectacular views

accompanied by qualified guides. A couple of informal local expat groups also run hikes around the emirate – see, for example, www.meetup.com/UAEtrekkers and www.meetup.com/Abu-Dhabi-Adventurers.

Horse and camel riding. The Arab love of horses is legendary, and riding is a popular pastime for many residents. Abu Dhabi Equestrian Club (Al-Mushrif; tel: 02-445 5500; www.emirates racing.com) is a large equestrian centre in the middle of Abu Dhabi Island. Further afield, the Dhabian Equestrian Club (tel: 050-134 7141), reached by heading north towards Dubai then taking the road east towards Ajban, offers instruction, rides and treks. For camel rides try Al Ain Camel Safaris, contactable via the Hilton Al Ain (tel: 03-768 8006).

Birdwatching. The greening of the desert in such a dry environment has greatly increased the variety and number of resident and visiting birds to the emirate (there are now about 220 species). Spring (Mar–May) and autumn (Aug–Nov) are particularly good times to observe birds migrating between wintering grounds in Africa and summer breeding habitats in Asia. Even in the city, any open parkland attracts spectacular birds, such as the distinctive hoopoe. The oases of Al Ain and Liwa are important resting points for birds flying across the Arabian Desert. For more information see www.uaebirding.com or the website of the Ornithological Society of the Middle East (www.osme.org).

INDOOR SPORTS

Health clubs and gyms. All the major hotels have fitness centres, and there are also several private health clubs. Al Wahda Health Club, at the Grand Millennium Hotel (Hazza bin Zayed St, Al Wahda; tel: 02 495 3831; www.millennium hotels.ae/grandmillenniumalwahda) is the largest in the city, with a huge gym plus sauna, steam room and Jacuzzi, closely followed by the Abu Dhabi Country Club (Al-Mushrif, entrance off Al-Saada Street; tel: 02-657 7777; www.adcountryclub.com), with all types of fitness equipment, ball courts, pools and exercise classes available. The long-running Hiltonia Health Club at the Hilton hotel in the centre (Corniche Rd; tel: 02 681 1900) is another popular choice, and also gets you access to the hotel's superb stretch of private beach.

Firing range. Shooting is particularly popular in the UAE: try your hand at the firing range at the Caracal Shooting Club (tel: 02-441 6404; www.caracalsc.ae) in the Armed Forces Officers' Club near the Grand Mosque. As a walk-in guest you will need passport ID, after which you choose from a range of pistols, semi-automatic weapons and bolt-action rifles.

Ten-pin bowling. Of the various ten-pin bowling alleys around the emirate, including the handily located Emirates Bowling Mall at the Marina Mall in Abu Dhabi City, the best is undoubtedly the 40-lane Khalifa International Bowling Centre (tel: 02-403 4200; www.zsc.ae) at Zayed Sports City. Scoring is fully computerised and coaching is available if required.

Ice-skating and skiing. Also at Zayed Sports City, the Abu Dhabi Ice Rink (tel: 02-403 4333) is the complete antidote to life in the hot city. The Olympic-sized rink can accommodate up to 400 skaters, and tuition is available. In Al Ain, there's the similarly impressive ice rink at the Al Ain Mall (tel: 03-766 0333; www.alainmall.net).

Indoor skydiving. Spacewalk at the Abu Dhabi Country Club (tel: 02 657 7777; www.adcountryclub.com) offers the chance to experience freefall flying.

SHOPPING

One of the attractions of a visit to Abu Dhabi is the huge number of retail outlets offering great-value shopping. Vast malls (usually open 10am–10pm, often later at weekends) are home to hundreds of shops, plus cafés, restaurants and other activities. Dominating the Breakwater area of Abu Dhabi City is the **Marina Mall** (tel: 02-681 8300 or 800 6623 (customer service); www.marinamall.ae). At the opposite end of the Corniche is **Abu Dhabi Mall** (tel: 02-645 4858; www.abudhabi-mall.com). Between the two and inland from the Corniche is the older-style **Madinat Zayed Shopping Centre** (tel: 02-633 3311; www.madinatzayed-mall.com) and a few blocks further east is the **Al-Wahda Mall** (tel: 02-443 7000; www.alwahda-mall.com). In Al Ain is the huge **Al Ain Mall** (tel: 03-766 0333; www.alainmall.net). Away from the malls are smaller independent shops that sell more unusual souvenirs such as wedding jewellery, metal coffee pots and traditional Omani daggers.

Marina Mall has over 400 shopping outlets

Gold and silver. Specialist shops sell good-quality gold and silver at great prices compared to Europe. Madinat Zayed Gold Souk is an older landmark in the heart of the city where gold is sold by weight, according to its price that day – bargaining is expected. One of the largest retailers is Damas Jewellery (www.damasjewel.com), with more than a dozen outlets in Abu Dhabi City.

Rugs and carpets. Abu Dhabi's proximity to the major carpet-producing regions of Persia, Turkey, Afghanistan and Kashmir means that the city is well-supplied with great-quality carpets and *kilims*. Most are good value, but it does pay to do a bit of homework and know what you are looking at. Many are factory manufactured, but there are some specialist shops selling handmade pieces. Try Red Sea Hand Made Carpets, which has outlets opposite the Madinat Zayed Gold Souk (tel: 02-633 3311) and behind the Al-Noor Hospital on Khalifa Street (tel: 02-626 6145). Another option is the Persian Carpets and Antiques Exhibition, at the Rotana Mall in Khalidiya (tel: 02-681 5900) and on the second floor of Marina Mall (tel: 02-681 6595).

Art, antiques and souvenirs. The Etihad Antique Gallery, opposite Abu Dhabi Mall (tel: 02-667 1229; www.ettihadgallery.com), usually has an interesting selection of pieces ranging from the 17th–20th centuries. The more downmarket Al Jaber Gallery (branches at the World Trade Center Central Market and on Yas Island; tel: 02-266 7700; www.aljabergallery.ae) is a decent place to pick up kitsch and inexpensive Arabian-style souvenirs – coffee pots, shisha pipes and so on. An offshoot of the excellent Dubai chain, Gallery One (Souk Qaryat al-Beri; tel: 02 558 1822, www.g-1.com) sells superb limited edition photographs of the city and emirates, along with superior postcards. In Al Ain, visit Royal Copper Antiques, Khalifa Street, opposite Medan City Market (tel: 03-766 1169).

Local crafts. A limited amount of craftwork is produced

Bargaining

Even if you don't like haggling over prices, it is all part of the buying process in smaller independent shops, especially when buying jewellery, carpets and souvenirs. As a rule, try to settle for something between a half and two-thirds of the initial price, or to get something extra for free. Prices in shopping malls are fixed.

Souvenirs for sale at the Heritage Village on the Breakwater

locally, including weaving, paintings and perfumes. The main outlets are the Heritage Village at the Breakwater and the Women's Handicraft Centre in Al-Mushrif (tel: 02-447 6645).

Books and publications. Shops and hotels sell coffee-table books about Abu Dhabi, Al Ain and the Emirates, but there are few specialist shops stocking detailed publications about the region. The Abu Dhabi Tourism and Culture Authority (ADACH; www.tcaabudhabi.ae/en) produces several detailed publications and magazines. Magrudy's (www.magrudy.com) has bookshops at Al-Wahda Mall in Abu Dhabi City, and at Al-Bawadi Mall in Al Ain.

ENTERTAINMENT

Most of Abu Dhabi's regular nightlife revolves around the numerous bars and nightclubs in the large hotels. Various venues host a variety of one-off concerts, theatrical and operatic performances. Check listings in hotels and local magazines.

A sunset dhow cruise

Bars and nightclubs. Hotel bars and clubs are all very different, from quiet and relaxed to noisy and lively. Alcoholic drinks can be quite pricey as a result of hefty government taxes, although many places run nightly happy hours, and regular Ladies' Nights at various establishment offer free tipples for the fairer sex. Popular bars include Sax at Le Royal Méridien, The Captain's Arms at Le Méridien, Brauhaus at the Beach Rotana and Paco's at the Al Ain Hilton. The terrace of the Yacht Bar at the Intercontinental has fabulous views across the marina at sunset. Some places strictly enforce dress codes, so keep it smart casual.

Live music. Look out for one-off concerts at the various venues. It could be Tom Jones rocking the crowds at Yas Island, Elton John at the Emirates Palace or Zubin Mehta conducting the Vienna Philharmonic at the Jahili Fort in Al Ain. Some hotel bars have live music, mostly jazz acts or perhaps a live DJ – the evergreen Jazz Bar at the Hilton is one of the best such venues, with live music most nights.

***Dhow* cruises.** A cruise aboard a traditional *dhow* as it sails along the Corniche provides a memorable view of the city's magnificent waterfront – sunset and dinner cruises are particularly popular. Reliable operators include Al Dhafra (tel: 02-444 9914, Net Tours (tel: 02-679 4656, www.nettoursuae.ae) and the long-running Shuja Yacht (tel: 050-695 0530), operated by Le Royal Méridien Hotel.

Cinemas. The latest Hollywood blockbuster is likely to be playing at a multiplex cinema in Abu Dhabi or Al Ain – www.timeoutabudhabi.com/films gives a convenient overview of what's currently showing in the city's various venues. Tickets are good value, although audiences can sometimes be distractingly noisy.

Art galleries. There's a burgeoning number of art galleries in Abu Dhabi, while the city also hosts the ever-growing Art Abu Dhabi annual art fair (see page 97). Leading venues include the Salwa Zeidan Gallery (www.salwazeidangallery.com), Ghaf Art Gallery (tel: 02 665 5332) and the 1x1 Gallery (www.1x1artgallery.com).

CHILDREN'S ABU DHABI

Abu Dhabians are very family-orientated, and children are welcomed across the country, with plenty of activities designed specifically for them. In such a hot and sunny climate, shaded **public parks** are extremely popular, particularly at the end of the day and evening. Every town and city has public parks (there are around twenty in Abu Dhabi City), some with slides, swings and climbing frames for children. All the large malls have dedicated kids' play areas including Fun City at Marina Mall, Kidoos at Abu Dhabi Mall, Wanasa Land at Al-Wahda Mall, and Candy Castle at Al Ain Mall.

The city's two blockbuster kids' attractions are both on Yas Island: the huge **Ferrari World** theme park (see page 42), and **Yas Waterworld** (www.yaswaterworld.com), a state-of-the-art waterpark offering all sorts of liquid thrills and spills. Other child-friendly attractions in and around Abu Dhabi City include the **Abu Dhabi Falcon Hospital** and **Saluki Dog Training Centre**, both located near the international airport. Nearby Al-Bahia (about 35km/22 miles from the city centre on the Dubai road) is home to **the Emirates Park Zoo** (www.emiratesparkzoo.com), where you will find exotic white tigers, lions, cheetahs and a Siberian bear, as well as a 'domestic section' where children can pet various different animals. In the city centre itself, Sheikh Khalifa Park, at the eastern end of the island, is home to a low-key **Aquarium** and the intriguing **'Time Tunnel'**, a gentle twenty-minute ride passing through various scenes from Abu Dhabi's history, brought to life with lots of animatronic waxworks and other props. Khalifa Park is also where you will find the modest but enjoyable Murjan Splash Park waterpark.

At Al Ain the main attraction is the **Al Ain Zoo**, where kids can get a close-up view of a host of interesting animals, including big cats, giraffes, rhinos and the ever-popular primates. North of Al Ain, **Hili Fun City** (tel: 03-784 5542, www.hilifuncity.ae; ladies-only on Wed) is a large amusement park reserved for families with children, with 20 different rides. East of Al Ain, beyond the Danat Al Ain Hotel, is the **Al Ain Raceway** (tel: 03-768 6662; www.alainraceway.com) where kids can race go-karts in three age categories: 8–11 years, 12–15 years and 16 plus.

Many hotels have child-friendly pool facilities

CALENDAR OF EVENTS

January Top golfers compete in the Abu Dhabi Golf Championships (www.abudhabigolfchampionship.com). Beginning of the traditional *dhow* racing season.

January–February Big Boys Toys Fair (www.bigboystoysuae.com) at ADNEC.

February Motorsports enthusiasts race up the world's tallest sand dune in the Moreeb Hill Climb. UAE President's Endurance Horse Race takes place over 160km (100 miles).

March The Abu Dhabi Festival (www.abudhabifestival.ae/en) features a varied programme of ballet, opera, classical and Arabic music.

April–May International Book Fair (www.adbookfair.com) at ADNEC. The Al-Gharbia Water Sports Festival (www.algharbiafestivals.com), based at Mirfa, includes kite-surfing, wake-boarding and surf-ski kayaking.

June–July Month of Ramadan (approximate dates: 27 May-25 June, 2017; 16 May-14 June, 2018; 6 May-4 June, 2019). Eid al-Fitr is a three-day celebration at the end of Ramadan.

June–August Abu Dhabi City Summer Festival, a six-week carnival.

July Liwa dates festival (www.liwadatesfestival.ae) at Mezaira.

September Hunting and Equestrian Exhibition (www.adihex.net).

October Abu Dhabi Film Festival (www.abudhabifilmfestival.ae).

November Formula 1 Grand Prix at Yas Island (www.yasmarinacircuit.com). Art Abu Dhabi contemporary art fair (www.abudhabiartfair.ae) and Art Abu Dhabi International Fair at ADNEC (www.emiratesartandantiquesfairs.com). Spectacular displays at the Al Ain Aerobatic Show (www.alainaerobaticshow.com).

December National Day comprises two days of sporting events, parades and celebrations. Al-Dhafra Festival (www.aldhafrafestival.ae) around Madinat Zayed City, Al-Gharbia, including a beauty contest for camels. The Mubadala World Tennis Championships (www.mubadalawtc.com) at Zayed Sports City see the world's top six players slugging it out on court.

EATING OUT

Abu Dhabi's location between Europe, Asia and Africa is reflected in the unusually wide range of cuisines on offer around the city, catering to the diverse tastes of locals, tourists and the huge number of expats who live here. Middle Eastern food is of course everywhere, while there's also a healthy selection of Persian, Indian, Mediterranean, Egyptian, African and Far Eastern flavours, served in a wide variety of settings ranging from swanky five-star hotel restaurants to unpretentious street cafés.

WHERE TO EAT

There are some great restaurants around Abu Dhabi, the best of which are generally found in the city's more upmarket hotels, employing top chefs and serving up high-quality cuisine, with prices to match. You don't have to be a guest at a hotel to use their restaurants, but you might need to make a reservation. Outside the hotels there are plenty of smaller independent restaurants and cafes where quality can be almost as high, and prices considerably lower. Indian food is particularly popular thanks to the city's large subcontinental expat population, and there are also plenty of Middle Eastern establishments serving up tasty kebabs and mezze, as well as Chinese, Vietnamese, Thai, European and other places. Note, however, that only hotel restaurants are allowed to serve alcohol. There are also an increasing number

Dates on the palm

of Western-style coffee shops, serving snacks, pastries and great coffee, while many of the international fast-food chains also have outlets here.

Outside Abu Dhabi City options are more limited, but even the smallest town will have a local restaurant or café open throughout the day.

Many hotels offer barbecue buffets at weekends

WHEN TO EAT

Breakfast timings in hotels tend to be quite extensive, roughly between 7am and 10am, while some local restaurants open even earlier (from 6am) to serve breakfast to the city's army of workers. Lunch is generally quite late, anywhere from 2pm to 5pm, after which some establishments close for the afternoon. Evening meals tend to be taken later and might not begin until 10pm, stretching way beyond midnight, and can become great family social occasions.

Hotels are mindful that Westerners and many tourists prefer to eat earlier, and serve food accordingly. Many restaurants offer Friday eat-all-you-want brunches or barbecue deals, which are extremely popular with families at weekends.

WHAT TO EAT

From the most expensive meal in a top hotel to street food enjoyed by families taking an evening stroll, the

Spectacular views from the terrace at the Mercure Jebel Hafeet

ingredients used are fresh and sometimes locally produced. The irrigation of great swathes of desert, especially in the Al-Gharbia region, has meant that plenty of locally cultivated vegetables and fresh fruit are available, as well as some meat and poultry. Abu Dhabi's position on the Gulf and closeness to the Indian Ocean assures a good supply of fish and seafood.

BREAKFAST

For most visitors, breakfast will be a large buffet provided by the hotel, usually with a huge choice of breads, pastries, salads, fruit and cold meats, as well as hot dishes made to order by a chef. Sometimes there will also be a typical Arab dish, perhaps *fuul*, made from broad fava beans, to be ladled out from a large steaming metal pot. *Fuul* comes in a wide variety of styles and is a popular and filling dish to start the day. *Fuul medammes* is seasoned with cumin, olive oil, lemon and spices, but there are always plenty of additional accompaniments, such as tomatoes, onions and peppers, to add to your own particular taste. Outside the hotels it's easiest to head for a local Western-style coffee shop for coffee and pastries.

An unusual local Arabian breakfast (although not recommended for calorie-conscious visitors) is *luqaimat*, consisting of fried batter dumplings covered with sweet date syrup eaten with a sweet noodle/omelette mixture, with the aid of *khubz khameer*, a local bread baked with spices.

LUNCH AND DINNER

Traditional Arabian lunch and dinner menus tend to be quite similar, starting with a few plates of appetisers or

RAMADAN

The fasting month of Ramadan throws working hours and mealtimes into disarray, especially outside of the hotels. The vast majority of Abu Dhabi's population are Muslims and do not eat, drink or smoke during daylight hours, but non-Muslims are permitted to use the restaurants and cafés that remain open within hotels. For non-Muslims it is prohibited to eat, drink or smoke outdoors in public, and alcohol is not sold, except for room service in the hotels. As soon as the sun sets everyone breaks the fast to eat the *iftar* meal, begin drinking and having fun, which can often carry on right through the night until the early-morning meal, the final one before daylight. There are often many additional after-dark social and culinary events organised during Ramadan, and you'll sometimes have the opportunity to sample local Emirati food, which is not often available at other times, so keep an eye out for communal meals offered at cultural, social or sporting centres as part of their special Ramadan activities.

Local breads

There are several types of Emirati bread, collectively called *khubz*. *Ragaag* is wafer-thin bread made from soft unleavened dough, sometimes served with a topping such as butter, cheese or meat. *Jabab* is thin and cooked on both sides like a pancake, also with added toppings, while *khameer* is a thick circular yeast bread.

mezze, which in themselves can be quite substantial. Many of these dishes originated in the Eastern Mediterranean, Lebanon in particular, and have now established themselves throughout the Arab world. *Tahini* is a thin paste made from ground sesame seeds with added olive oil and spices, whilst *babaganoush* is mashed aubergine with garlic, lemon juice and oil. *Moutabbal* is made from roasted aubergines and sesame paste, while *hummus*, made from chickpeas, garlic and oil, is popular and readily available worldwide. *Fatoush* is a salad made from tomato and pieces of pitta bread, while *tabouleh* is cracked wheat, tomato and parsley. *Kibbeh* are small deep-fried balls of minced meat, wheat and pine nuts, and are perfect when a full meal is too much.

A popular lunchtime dish is lamb, chicken or shrimp *makboos*. The main ingredient is cooked slowly throughout the morning with onions and saffron rice, then seasoned with spices and lime, after which seasonal vegetables, such as tomatoes, green peppers or potatoes, are added. Main dishes for both lunch and dinner include the Indian-inspired fish *biryani* – rice, spices, vegetables and seafood all cooked together, and *laham mashwee* – stuffed lamb eaten with bread. *Kuftah* are meatball kebabs rolled up in pitta bread with salad and yogurt, and *samak bilfern* is baked fish with added spices, served with lime, salad and rice. Many places offer main-meal menus with standard dishes such as grilled meats, fish, kebabs and chicken, served with different varieties of rice, as well as pasta dishes.

SNACKS

Throughout the day, delicious snacks can be bought around every corner, whether from a trendy WiFi café or a street food vendor. A delicious *falafel* sandwich is a great standby for vegetarians, made from deep-fried patties of mashed chickpeas and parsley, placed into an envelope of local bread with finely chopped mixed salad, *tahini* or hummus, and sometimes pickles. Giant skewers of grilled lamb meat, known as *shawarma* sliced into a kebab are a great option when eating on the move. Some local eateries lure in passers-by with their succulent rotisserie chickens slow cooking in ovens set up on the pavement outside and are usually cheap and cheerful places for a quick meal.

Baking bread at the Shangri-La Hotel

Chef preparing food at an Abu Dhabi restaurant

EMIRATI CUISINE

True Emirati food is most likely to be created in private households and is difficult to find in restaurants. Two options are the Heritage Village on the Breakwater, which sometimes serves Emirati dishes on a Friday evening, and the Al-Arish restaurant at Al-Mina Port, which serves Emirati-style spiced fish. There are also sometimes opportunities to sample local cuisine during the nightly *iftar* buffets served during the month of Ramadan, or during the Eid al-Fitr celebrations at the end of the month. If you are lucky enough to be invited to a wedding or special celebration, you might see traditional dishes served on a large platter, with diners sitting around it on the floor. When instructed by your hosts, dig in, but make sure you use only your right hand.

One of the favourite meals is *harees*, a kind of porridge made from pieces of meat and wheat. The wheat is cooked in a pot then the meat is added and left for another few hours. This mixture is then transferred to an oven (or buried under hot coals if in the desert) and cooked for a few more hours until ready to serve. Another special dish is *thareed*, made from a spicy meat and vegetable stew, poured over thin *ragaag* bread.

Khouzi is the celebratory meal of Arabian Bedouins, where a whole lamb (or sometimes a young camel) is stuffed with rice, eggs, onions, fruit and nuts. Sometimes the ingredients are placed inside a chicken, which is then inserted into the lamb or camel. The entire animal is then baked until the meat is tender enough to drop from the bone. It is usually served on giant platters as chunks of meat lying on a bed of rice and other ingredients, into which everyone digs with their right hand.

DESSERTS

Om Ali (meaning the 'mother of Ali') is a delicious and filling pudding, presented in a hot baking pot. It is made from milk, nuts, dried fruit, coconuts, cinnamon and cream, separated by layers of thin corn bread. *Muhalabiya* is a sugary milk pudding served with pistachio nuts and rose

TRADITIONAL EMIRATI FOOD

The nature of a traditional Emirati meal depends on whether you imagine yourself with the fishing families living in a *barasti* palm shelter on the seashore or with the Bedouins of the desert.

Along the coast the locals would catch fish, seafood and even dugong (now protected). In the old days, before refrigeration and freezing, plentiful supplies meant that there was a great tradition of grilling, frying and baking fish. An ideal way to use surplus fish was to dry it, but the resultant meals struggled to get much of the flavour back.

Inland the staple diet would have been dates, milk and, very rarely, camel meat. Camel would only be served up on really special occasions, as the animals were far too valuable to be killed just for their meat – they provided transport, milk and wealth for the entire family.

Enjoying a shisha water pipe at the Emirates Palace Hotel

water. A large number of patisseries and cake shops are spread across the city, and many of the sweet sticky pastries will be familiar from Greece, Turkey or Lebanon. *Baklava* is a light filo pastry stuffed with honey and pistachio nuts, while *kunafa* is similar but made with a more delicate shredded pastry. *Basboosa* is a semolina cake, dripping with syrup and lemon.

DRINKING AND SMOKING

The only place to get an alcoholic drink in Abu Dhabi is at one of the international hotels or members' clubs (including golf clubs), where the restaurants, bars and nightclubs are often lively, especially at weekends. There are many international-style coffee shops all over the city, serving the usual range of cappuccinos, lattes, mochas, macchiatos and so on.

The communal smoking of a *shisha* (also known as a *nargile* or hubbly-bubbly) water pipe has regained popularity and can be tried in many restaurants and cafés. The tobacco itself is usually thick and pungent, and often mixed with other flavours such as molasses, mint, apple and other fruits. This activity is not just confined to old men, as it is quite common to see a group of youngsters of both sexes sharing a *shisha* in one of the open-air restaurants along the Corniche.

TO HELP YOU ORDER

Do you have a table, please? **Andak taawila, men fadlak?**
Bon appetit! **Sahtain!**
The bill, please. **Fattoura, men fadlak.**
I would like... **Ana areed...**

apple **toofa**
aubergine **baleyan**
beans **fuul**
beer **beera**
bread **khubz**
butter **samn**
cheese **jibna**
chicken **dajaj**
chickpeas **hummus**
chocolate **shokalata**
coffee **gahwa**
eggs **baith**
fish **samak**
liver **kibdah**
meat **lahm**
without meat **bidun laham**
meatballs **kuftah**
milk **haleeb**
olives **zaytoun**
onions **basal**
oranges **burtogal**
pasta **makaruna**
pepper **filfil**
pineapple **ananas**
potato **batata**
prawns/shrimps **gambari/rubian**
rice **ruz**
salad **salata**
salt **milh**
soup **shorbah**
sugar **shakkar**
tea **shai**
tomatoes **tamat**
vinegar **khall**
water **maya**
watermelon **jeh**
wine **nabeeth**

PLACES TO EAT

We have used the following symbols to give an idea of the price for a three-course meal for one:

$$$$** over 500 Dhs **$$ 125 to 250 Dhs
$$$** 250 to 500 Dhs **$ up to 125 Dhs

DOWNTOWN ABU DHABI

Al-Dhafra $$$ *Al-Mina Port, tel: 02-673 2266,* www.aldhafra.net. One of the most memorable ways to see the city is from the water, and this evening dinner cruise (departing at 8.30pm, returning at 10.30pm) is a lovely opportunity to watch the city buildings and lights float past. The size of the *dhow* depends on the number of guests that evening; the small boat can take as few as six. At the dockside there is also the Al-Mina coffee shop and the Al-Arish fish restaurant, offering Emirati-style cuisine. Does not always operate, especially in summer, so check in advance.

BiCE $$$ *Jumeirah at Etihad Towers hotel, Corniche, tel: 02-811 5666.* Classy Italian restaurant, relocated to the swanky Jumeirah at Etihad Towers hotel. The menu features a mix of classic and modern Italian fare, immaculately prepared and bursting with fresh flavours, including pastas, pizzas, risottos, plus meat and seafood mains. Open for lunch and dinner.

Chamas $$$ *Intercontinental, Bainunah Street, tel: 02-666 6888,* www.dining-intercontinental-ad.ae. Lively Brazilian *churrascaria*-style eatery with as much meat as you can eat, cooked and served on skewers. A live band plays Latin rhythms, making every night like a carnival. Next door, the chic Yacht Club Bar attracts the city's smart set and is a great place for a drink before or after a meal. Open evenings only, plus Fri brunch.

Finz $$$$ *Beach Rotana, Tourist Club Area, tel: 02-697 9000,* www.rotana.com/beachrotana. One of the city's top seafood restaurants, set in an unusual wooden structure jutting out over the beach with fine views over the water to the ever-expanding developments on Mariyah Island. Fish is cooked in a variety of international styles, ranging from wok to tandoori. Open for lunch and dinner.

Hakkasan $$$$ *Emirates Palace hotel, tel: 02-690 7730,* www.emiratespalace.com. This is a flamboyant, super-swanky offshoot of the famous London restaurant. Opulent decor is combined with fine-dining contemporary Chinese cuisine, including beautiful dim sum. Open for dinner daily, plus lunch on Fri & Sat.

Havana Café $$ *Opposite Marina Mall, tel: 02-681 0044.* Very popular venue at which workers and shoppers meet up at the end of the day for good café food, snacks, cakes, pastries, drinks and lots of shisha – although service can be hit and miss. There is a large open area with great views across the Breakwater to the Corniche. Open until 1am.

Ibrahimi Restaurant $ *Electra (7th) St, Al Markaziyah, tel: 02-634 4244,* www.alibrahimirestaurant.com. A small local venue serving great-value Indian and Persian cuisine. The menu is mind-boggling, the service is quick and the food is delicious. There is a second branch behind the main Post Office at Madinat Zayed Shopping Centre. Open for lunch and dinner.

India Palace $$ *Al-Salam Street, about 400m/yds from Abu Dhabi Mall, tel: 02-644 8777,* www.indiapalace.ae. Popular Indian cuisine served all day in a great downtown location, close to all the action. Another of the longer-established restaurants, busy with office workers at lunchtime and a great choice for an evening away from the large hotels. Open for lunch and dinner.

Indigo $$$ *Beach Rotana hotel, Tourist Club Area, tel: 02-697 9011,* www.rotana.com/beachrotana. Smart but affordable Indian restaurant, with superior decor and a nice selection of North Indian classics done with contemporary flair – try the signature Sikandari raan: roasted lamb stuffed with prunes, onions and cheese. Open for lunch and dinner.

Lebanese Flower $$ *Khalidiyah branch, tel: 02-665 8700; Defence Road branch, tel: 02-642 4208.* Great Middle-Eastern food and a good choice of *mezzes*, *shawarmas* and juices, all served in large portions. Both outlets are always crowded and popular with local Emirati families and expat Arabs. Takeaway available. Open for lunch and dinner.

The One Restaurant $$ *Sheikh Zayed the First Street, Khalidiyah, tel: 02-681 6500,* www.theone.com. Tucked away inside the trendy The One interior design store, this funky little café is amongst the more consistently popular in town, serving up tasty and health-conscious bistro fare with an international range of flavours. Open daily 8am–9pm (Fri 10am–9pm).

Quest $$$$ *Jumeirah at Etihad Towers hotel, Corniche, tel: 02-811 5666,* www.jumeirah.com. On the 63rd floor of the futuristic Jumeirah Etihad Towers, Quest serves up some of the city's highest and most jaw-dropping views alongside excellent Pan-Asian food blending Chinese, Japanese and Malaysian influences and including lots of speciality wok dishes. Open for lunch and dinner.

Rodeo Grill $$$$ *Beach Rotana hotel, Tourist Club Area, tel: 02-697 9011,* www.rotana.com/beachrotana. Abu Dhabi's oldest steakhouse, and arguably still its best, with prime cuts of US Angus and Australian *wagyu* served, as well as other meat dishes and some seafood. Open for lunch and dinner.

Samurai $$ *Al-Mina Road (next to Al-Diar Capital Hotel), tel: 02-676 6612,* www.samurai.ae. Located between the Tourist Club Area and the Corniche, this place serves unpretentious Japanese food in a chintzy, bright-red dining room. There is a huge choice of fresh, well-presented maki, sushi, sashimi, teppanyaki and yakiniku – raw pieces of meat or seafood that you grill at your table. Open for lunch and dinner.

Tiara $$$ *Marina Mall, tel: 02-681 9090.* The food from Tiara's European quasi fine-dining menu is not likely to set your pulse racing, but the views from this revolving restaurant most certainly will, with sweeping vistas across the city and along the coast from the top of the tower above Marina Mall. Open for lunch and dinner. Reservations recommended.

Le Vendôme $$$$ *Emirates Palace, Corniche, tel: 02-690 7999,* www.emiratespalace.com. One of the most popular restaurants in the Emirates Palace, which raises the bar of the traditional international buffet with a wonderful selection of freshly cooked quality food for breakfast, lunch and dinner. Dine inside or along the breezy terrace with views across the beach and lagoon. Try a slice of the famous Emirates Palace Cake, decorated with edible gold. Open for breakfast, lunch and dinner.

MAINLAND ABU DHABI CITY

Bord Eau $$$$ *Shangri-La hotel, tel: 02-509 8511,* www.shangri-la.com/AbuDhabi. One of the top European-style restaurants in town, serving up modern French haute cuisine in a rather stately European-style dining room – choose from a short menu of meat and fish mains, all beautifully presented. Open for dinner only.

Rangoli $$$–$$$$ *Yas Island Rotana, Yas Island, tel: 02-656 4000,* www.rotana.com/yasislandrotana. One of several highly rated restaurants at this swish hotel, serving fine modern north and south Indian cuisine in a chic dining room with acres of stripped-down dark wood. Open for dinner only.

Shang Palace $$$$ *Shangri-La Hotel and Resort, Qaryat al-Beri, Between the Bridges, tel: 02-509 8503,* www.shangri-la.com. One of several fine restaurants in the stunning Shangri-La, Shang Palace specializes in top-notch Chinese cooking with specialities from across the country served in a lavishly decorated setting. Open for lunch and dinner.

Ushna $$$ *Qaryat al-Beri, tel: 02-558 1769.* Stylish modern restaurant opposite the waterfront, with lovely views across to the Grand Mosque. Food features innovative contemporary interpretations of classic North Indian dishes, and there is also an impressive drinks list. Open for lunch and dinner.

AL AIN

Eden Rock $$$ *Mercure Grand Hotel Jebel Hafeet, tel: 03-783 8888,* www.mercure.com. The open terrace at the Eden Rock looks down across the barren mountainside to the lights of Al Ain far below, while the adjoining terrace café, just a few steps away from the pool, has truly spectacular views at night. Food is à la carte during the week, and buffet at weekends, with a range of international offerings – although it's the views that really impress. Open for lunch and dinner.

Flavours $$$ *Hilton Hotel, Al-Sarooj District, tel: 03-768 6666,* www3.hilton.com. This place keeps it simple, with tasty food at good prices. Both the cuisine and interior decor are Arab-inspired, while food has international influences, including regular Asian, American, seafood and other theme nights. Open for breakfast, lunch and dinner.

Heritage Village $ *Al-Qatara Oasis, tel: 03-763 0155.* Located amidst the lush palms of Al-Qatara Oasis on the northern edge of Al Ain, this traditional restaurant is tricky to find but offers a welcome alternative to yet another hotel restaurant, with traditional decor and a menu of tasty and inexpensive Arabian fare, plus shisha, attracting a mainly Emirati crowd. Open for lunch and dinner.

Min Zaman $$$ *Al Ain Rotana, tel: 03-754 5111,* www.rotana.com/alainrotana. Stylish Lebanese restaurant with Arabian Nights decor and a good selection of authentic meze and grills, plus shisha. A singer, belly-dancer and *oud* player perform nightly. You have a choice of seating either inside or on the terrace overlooking the garden. Open for dinner only.

Trader Vic's $$$ *Rotana Hotel, tel: 03-754 5111,* www.rotana.com/alainrotana. A relaxing, atmospheric bar-restaurant with a vaguely French Polynesian theme, a wide-ranging menu of international mains and some of the most potent cocktails in the UAE. Usually lively with a party crowd, especially at weekends, while special themed events and offers keep things busy. Open lunch and dinner.

LIWA

Al Waha $$$ *Qasr al Sarab hotel, tel: 02 886 2088,* www.qasralsarab.anantara.com. This is the suave all-day dining restaurant at the stunning Qasr al Sarab desert resort, Al Waha ('The Oasis'). The restaurant serves up a superb spread of international food with a decided Arabian flavour, including grill stations turning out superb meats and seafood. Open for lunch and dinner.

MIRFA

Manara Al Marfa $$ *Mirfa Hotel, tel: 02-883 3030,* www.almarfapearlhotels.com/mirfa. Situated in the large atrium below reception, this bright and airy restaurant opens out onto the pool and beach, with fabulous views out to sea. International à la carte and buffet choices for lunch and dinner. The restaurant and bar are the social hub for expat workers in the area and get lively most nights.

JEBEL DHANNA

Zaitoun $$ *Danat Jebel Dhanna Resort, tel: 02-801 2222,* www.danathotels.com. Small, intimate and beautifully decorated restaurant offering a decent stab at authentic Italian cuisine in the depths of Al-Gharbia, with good home-made pasta, nourishing meat and seafood mains plus the inevitable tiramisu and panna cotta.

SIR BANI YAS

Al Shams $$$$ *Desert Islands Resort and Spa, tel: 02-801 5400,* www.anantara.com. Of the resort's eight dining areas, the choice location has to be the Al Shams (Arabic for the Sun) beachside place. The restaurant is light and open, with tables overlooking the infinity pool and beach, and there is a quiet, intimate atmosphere. Fish and meat dishes of the highest quality are prepared nearby on an open fire. For special occasions, the hotel can arrange a private outdoor meal on one of the deserted beaches, or further inland amongst the rugged, multicoloured hills.

A–Z TRAVEL TIPS

A Summary of Practical Information

A

ACCOMMODATION (see also list of Recommended Hotels)

The overall quality of hotels in Abu Dhabi city is high, with a good range of top-end places as well as a growing number of less expensive establishments – although you're unlikely to find anywhere for less than around $65/night. It is obviously a good idea to book as far in advance as possible, especially if you're anxious to stay in a particular hotel, though there's generally plenty of accommodation available across the city even during big events like the F1 Grand Prix. Outside Abu Dhabi city, accommodation is much thinner on the ground, with only a few places to stay in the second city of Al Ain, and none at all in many other parts of the Emirate.

Walk-in rates can be very expensive; book online for the best deals. Belonging to a hotel frequent-visitor programme can also help. There are some real bargains to be had in the off-peak (summer) season, or when hotels have recently opened. Inclusive deals with flights and hotel can be much better value than buying the flight and accommodation separately. There are some serviced apartments for longer stays or as an alternative to hotel rooms.

When you see ++ after an advertised price it means that you need to add on 10 percent service charge and 6 percent tourism fee. Credit cards are accepted everywhere.

hotel **funduq/hotel**
How much? **Bi kum?**

AIRPORT

The main arrivals point is Abu Dhabi International Airport (AUH; www.abudhabiairport.ae). National carrier Etihad Airways now has its own dedicated Terminal Three. Those requiring visas can purchase them before immigration. The downtown hotels are about 35km (20 miles) away, but taxis seldom take longer than 45 minutes, except during rush-hour periods. A taxi from the airport to the city centre costs around 80–95 Dhs; alternatively, airport bus A1 runs regularly into the centre (every 40 minutes; 4 Dhs). If flying with Etihad or one of eleven other airlines, baggage can be dropped 4–24 hours before departure at the City Air Terminal (tel: 02-644 8434) in the Tourist Club Area (www.abudhabiairport.ae – 'Remote Check-In' is listed under Airport Information in the Airport Services section). There is no departure tax to pay.

B

BICYCLE AND MOTORCYCLE HIRE

The Corniche has cycle lanes running the full length of the city seafront. A range of street and mountain bikes are available from FunRideSports (tel: 02-445 5838, www.funridesports.com) which has four rental outlets along the Corniche boardwalk (main office outside The Hiltonia Beach Club opposite the Hilton Hotel). There is also a network of cycling paths running around Yas Island where you'll find another branch of FunRideSports. Any visit to Sir Bani Yas is incomplete without a mountain-bike ride around the north of the island, which is arranged at the resort.

You can also hire a Harley-Davidson motorbike for the day, week or month from Harley-Davidson Abu Dhabi (located out of town in the industrial suburb of Musafah, tel: 02-554 0667, www.harley-davidson.ae).

BOAT HIRE

A popular excursion from Abu Dhabi City, especially at weekends, is to take a boat from one of the many city marinas and head to one of the peaceful offshore islands. Hiring a boat privately can be expensive, so another way to get out onto the sea is to take a trip on one of the commercial *dhows*, which operate late afternoon/sunset pleasure cruises, sometimes including an evening meal. A full list of operators can be found on the tourist board website (www.visitabudhabi.ae – under the 'What to do' tab, then follow the 'Explore our waters' link).

BUDGETING FOR YOUR TRIP

Abu Dhabi benefits from good-value flights from major European airports, especially through its own Etihad Airways. The following prices in Dhs (UAE dirhams) will give a rough idea of how much you will spend. See Accommodation for details on hotel pricing and taxes.

Flights: return flights from the UK start at around £400.

Taxis: trips within downtown Abu Dhabi City (3km/2 miles): 20–30 Dhs; from one end of the city to the other, such as from the Corniche to Sheikh Zayed Grand Mosque (10km/6 miles): 40 Dhs.

Hotel: this is likely to be your largest expense, costing from around 225 Dhs in the very cheapest places up to 1,500 Dhs or more per night in the very best hotels.

Meals: set lunch/dinner or buffet in a four/five-star hotel 100–300 Dhs; lunch/dinner in a downtown restaurant 75–150 Dhs.

Drinks: Coffee 10–20 Dhs. You can buy a soft drink can in a supermarket or coffee from a streetside cafe for 1 Dh; in a cheap restaurant they usually cost about 5 Dh; in a five star hotel it might cost you 15–25 Dhs. Bottle of house wine 150–300 Dhs. Draught beer 30–40 Dhs. Measure of spirits 30–50 Dhs.

Sightseeing: cultural, government-run attractions like the Sheikh Zayed Mosque and Heritage Village (as well as the museums and forts in Al Ain) are either free or charge a nominal fee of around 5 Dhs. Privately run, family-oriented attractions like Ferrari World and Yas Waterworld are contrastingly expensive at around 270 Dhs. **Internet cafés:** 5–10 Dhs per hour.

C

CAMPING

There are no official campsites with toilet and washing facilities in Abu Dhabi, but spending the night amid the peaceful sand dunes is a popular pastime. Those spending a night in the open should take all equipment with them (including mobile phones and GPS) and ensure that they leave no rubbish behind. Overnight camping tours can be organised by desert safari operators, with all the infrastructure and equipment provided.

CAR HIRE (also see Driving)

A rented car or 4x4 vehicle can be the best way to reach the oases of Al Ain and Liwa or to explore the western coast. If staying within Abu Dhabi City, having a car is often more of a problem than a help, due to the busy streets and scarcity of parking places. Daily rates start at around $60/day for an economy car, rising to over $150/day for a big 4WD capable of going off road. Hiring a car with a driver costs roughly double, but is worthwhile if you need local knowledge. To hire a car you will need your passport, a credit card and either your driving licence from home or an international driving licence.

Numerous international chains have offices across the city including Avis (www.avis.com), Dollar Rent a Car (www.dollaruae.com), Europcar (www.europcar-abudhabi.com), Hertz (www.hertzuae.com), Fast (www.fastuae.com) and Thrifty (www.thriftyuae.com). Reliable local companies include Al-Ghazal, the transport arm of the National Hotel company (tel: 02-634 2200, www.adnh.com) and Eurostar Rental (tel: 03-876 7827, www.eurostarrental.com). Budget, Dollar, Europcar, Hertz and

Thrifty all have offices at the airport (see www.abudhabiairport.ae, 'To and From the Airport' for full details). Avis, Fast and Thrifty also have offices in Al Ain.

CLIMATE

Abu Dhabi has a subtropical climate, characterised by warm days and clear sunny skies. The winter months (Oct–Apr) are the most pleasant, and though some rainfall might occur, it is rarely more than a brief shower. Winter daytime temperatures are up to 25°C (77°F), with cool nights down to 10°C (50°F), but during the summer (May to September) it can get as hot as 48°C (118°F), with hot nights. Humidity is high along the coast, which can make summer rather uncomfortable. Inland the air is drier, so despite the higher temperatures it can feel more pleasant here in summer. Rainstorms are unusual, but can occur in winter.

	J	F	M	A	M	J	J	A	S	O	N	D
°C	19	20	23	27	32	34	35	36	33	30	25	21
°F	66	68	73	80	90	93	95	97	91	86	77	70

CLOTHING

Tourists should dress conservatively in towns and cities, and loose-fitting clothes made from natural fibres are ideal year-round. Swimwear is acceptable on the beach and inside resort complexes, but topless bathing is illegal. Visitors to the Grand Mosque must wear modest, loose clothing with long sleeves and long skirts or trousers, and women should wear a headscarf, which can be borrowed at the entrance. Bring a sunhat, high-factor sun cream and sunglasses, plus comfortable walking shoes for the desert. In winter, bring a fleece or jacket, as winds can be cold in the desert, at sea or at altitude on Jebel Hafeet. Most hotels and resorts have dress codes for their restaurants and bars, even down to forbidding open-toed sandals. Smart casual is recommended for any meal or drink out.

CRIME AND SAFETY

One of the main benefits of living in Abu Dhabi is the general feeling of safety. Despite this, be wary of pickpockets in crowded places such as bars, and do not leave valuables unattended when swimming. If anything is stolen, report it immediately to a police station (see page 127) and obtain a report for insurance purposes. The main safety concern is the risk of traffic accidents, so always use pedestrian crossings and observe the signs.

D

DRIVING (see also Car Hire)

Driving in Abu Dhabi is on the right, but parking is a real problem downtown and the quality of driving is a concern. Within Abu Dhabi City, traffic is usually too congested to build up much momentum, but out in the desert roads can often be dangerous, with locals driving at recklessly high speeds, especially along the road to Al Ain and the notorious Dubai highway. Always drive defensively and get out of the way if a vehicle approaches at speed. Don't make any hand gestures that might be construed as insulting, something punishable by law in the UAE. Using a hand-held mobile phone while driving is illegal, and those in the front seats must wear seat belts.

E

ELECTRICITY

Electricity supply is reliable and uses a 220–240v/50Hz current. Most European appliances work fine, but US devices on 110v require a transformer. Sockets are mainly square three-pin UK standard, but some US-run hotels are two-pin. Many electrical items are imported and sold with round two-pin plugs, but adaptors are readily available.

EMBASSIES AND CONSULATES

Australia: 8th Floor, Al-Muhairy Centre, Sheikh Zayed the First Street, Abu Dhabi, tel: 02-401 7500, www.uae.embassy.gov.au.

Canada: Abu Dhabi Trade Towers (Abu Dhabi Mall), West Tower, 9th and 10th floors, Abu Dhabi, tel: 02-694 0300, www.canadainternational.gc.ca/uae-eau.

Ireland: 1 & 2 Khalifa Al Suwaidi Development, Road 19, off 32nd Street, Al Bateen, Abu Dhabi, tel: 02-495 8200, www.embassyofireland.ae.

New Zealand: Villa 226/2, Al Karamah St (24th, between 11th and 13th Streets), Al Karamah, Abu Dhabi, tel: 02 441 1222, www.nzembassy.com/united-arab-emirates.

South Africa: Corner of Airport Road and 25th Street, Villa Number 202, tel: 02-447 3446, www.southafrica.ae.

UK Embassy: Khalid bin Al-Waleed St, Dubai, tel: 02-610 1100, www.ukinuae.fco.gov.uk.

United States: Street No. 4, off Al Karamah St, Al Karamah, Abu Dhabi, tel: 02-414 2200, http://abudhabi.usembassy.gov.

EMERGENCIES

With almost all of Abu Dhabi within mobile phone range, your first call should be **999** to alert all the emergency services – police, fire or ambulance. If involved in a road accident you must not leave the scene or move vehicles until the police have arrived. In case of an emergency while driving along the roads outside of Abu Dhabi City, call 02-604 4600. Emergency telephone numbers are:

Police: **999**
Ambulance: **999**
Fire: **997**
Coastguard: **996**

G

GAY AND LESBIAN TRAVELLERS

Homosexuality is technically illegal in Abu Dhabi, but some couples do have same-sex relationships. Gay and lesbian visitors will encounter few problems as long as they are discreet and cautious about any outward signs of affection towards each other. Local men often greet others with kisses and hold hands, but this is not the sign of a gay relationship.

GETTING THERE (see also Tourist Information)

By air. National carrier Etihad Airways' (www.etihad.com) operates direct flights from Abu Dhabi International Airport to London Heathrow, Manchester, Dublin, New York, Washington, Chicago and Toronto. British Airways also have direct flights between the UK and Abu Dhabi all year round. The international airport at Al Ain has flights mostly to the Indian subcontinent.

By road. Abu Dhabi shares border crossings with Oman at Al Ain (in the suburb of Hili) and Saudi Arabia, in the far west of the emirate, in the unlikely event that you enter the UAE from that direction. The same visa rules apply as when entering by air and assuming your paperwork is in order (as well as that of any vehicle you're bringing into the country) the whole procedure should not take more than half an hour or so.

By sea. An increasing number of cruise ships are stopping in Abu Dhabi as part of weekly cruises around the Gulf, or longer worldwide itineraries.

GUIDES AND TOURS

Daily city excursions and desert safaris operated by tour companies are always accompanied by qualified guides, while tour agencies can provide a vehicle, driver and guide for excursions to Liwa or Al-Gharbia lasting any number of days, as well as guided 4x4 safaris, trekking, riding and supervised camping in the desert. Recommended companies include:

Cyclone Tours: tel: mobile 050 622 5385, www.cyclonetours.com.

Desert Adventures Tourism: tel: 02 556 6155, www.desertadventures.com.

Emirates Tours: tel: 02-491 2929, www.eatours.ae.

Net Tours: tel: 02-679 4656, www.nettoursuae.com.

Orient Tours: tel: 04-282 8238, www.orient-tours-uae.com

Travco: tel: 055 760 3759, www.travcogroup.com.

H

HEALTH AND MEDICAL CARE

The standard of both government and private healthcare in Abu Dhabi is generally excellent, with top-class medical facilities. Apart from emergency treatment all medical costs have to be paid for, so comprehensive health insurance is recommended.

Most tourist illnesses are temporary, seldom lasting more than 24 hours. Stomach upsets are the most common, often due to dehydration, unclean water or change of environment. Too much sun can also cause problems, so always wear a sunhat and sunglasses, and use high-factor sun cream. Drink bottled water and avoid food that is not freshly cooked or has been lying around for a long time. Bring enough personal medicines with you, but be aware that some drugs are restricted within Abu Dhabi and the UAE (see page 132).

No vaccinations are compulsory, but polio, tetanus, typhoid and hepatitis A and B are recommended. For more information check www.mdtravelhealth.com.

Help me! **Saedni!**
Call a doctor! **Ottlub daktour!**

For less serious ailments, there are plenty of modern pharmacies for quick, professional advice and medicines. Hotels can always contact an English-speaking doctor or locate an open pharmacy. Try the Al-Noor 24 Hour Pharmacy, tel: 02-406 6933.

The city's best A&E department is at Sheikh Khalifa Medical City, tel: 02-819 0000, www.skmc.ae. There is also an A&E department at the Al-Noor Hospital, tel: 02-626 5265, www.alnoorhospital.com. Al Ain has the Tawam Hospital (managed by Johns Hopkins Medical International), tel: 03-767 7444, www.tawamhospital.ae.

L

LANGUAGE

Arabic is the official language, but English is widely understood, and most signs (including road signs) are usually in both languages. The large numbers of migrant workers means that Persian, Urdu, Hindi and several other Indian languages are also commonly used. In the hotels and resorts almost everything is done in both Arabic and English.

Some useful Arabic words and phrases:

yes/no **na'am/la**
hello/greeting **as-salam aleykum**
(response to hello) **wa-aleykum salam**
hello/welcome **ahlan wa sahlan/marhaba**
OK **tayib**
please **men fadlak**
thank you **shukran**
(response to thank you) **afwan**
how are you? **ish halak?**
I am fine **al-humdullilah**

good morning **sabah al-kher**
good evening **masa al-kher**
goodbye **ma'a salama/ fi aman illah**
what is your name? **shuw izmak?**
my name is... **izmi...**
I do not understand **mabfahem**
do you speak English? **tetkallam inglizi?**
market **souk**
mosque **masjed**

M

MAPS

New buildings and roads appear so fast that the latest maps go out of date quickly. The best – and usually most up-to-date – maps of the city and emirate are those produced by Explorer Publishing, including the useful *Abu Dhabi Map and Abu Dhabi Mini-Map*. The *Insight Travel Map* to *Oman and UAE* has a good Abu Dhabi City plan.

MEDIA

Newspapers, radio and television channels are all now established in Abu Dhabi. Most hotels and homes are fitted with satellite receivers to get hundreds of channels.

Abu Dhabi TV is an Arabic-language network with its sister channels Emirates TV. The Sports Channel shows live events from around the world, including the English Premier League.

The English-language daily newspaper of Abu Dhabi is *The National*, whose website (www.thenational.ae) is a great way to keep up to date with events. Two English-language papers from Dubai are *Gulf News* (www.gulfnews.com) and *Khaleej Times* (www.khaleej times.ae). Abu Dhabi Week (www.abudhabiweek.ae) comes out every Thursday with good information and listings, while monthly magazines *Time Out Abu Dhabi*, *What's On Abu Dhabi* and *Concierge* provide knowledgeable local coverage.

The English-language station Emirates Radio 1 on 100.5FM plays the latest rock and pop, while Emirates Radio 2 on 106.0FM plays older classics. The BBC World Service broadcasts in Arabic and English at 90.3FM.

MONEY

The UAE's currency is the Dirham (abbreviated to Dhs, Dh or AED), divided into 100 fils (although these are now hardly ever used). Dirham currency notes are 1,000, 500, 200, 100, 50, 20, 10 and 5 Dhs, below which there are coins for 1 Dhs, 50 fils and 25 fils. The Dirham is pegged to the US dollar at a rate of 10 Dhs to 2.72 USD. Dirhams can be purchased overseas and brought into the country.

Currency exchange. Most costs during a visit can be paid by credit card, or you can get local cash from one of the many ATM machines. All the main shopping malls have efficient money exchanges offering good rates and are open much longer than banks. Hotels usually offer poor exchange rates. Traveller's cheques can occasionally be a problem to exchange, requiring proof of purchase and ID, with higher commissions charged.

O

OPENING HOURS

The public sector has already switched from the traditional Thursday and Friday weekend to a Friday and Saturday weekend, and many, but not all, offices and businesses have followed this change.

Banks: 8am–2pm Sun–Thur (some are also open same hours on Saturdays, plus late afternoon 4.30–6.30pm). Closed Fri and holidays.

Business: 8am–1pm and 4pm–7pm, but some remain open through the day. Closed Fri and holidays.
Government offices: 7.30am–2pm. Closed Fri and holidays.
Shopping malls: 10am–10pm daily, often staying open later Thur–Sat.
Smaller shops: generally 7am–10pm, but often closed through the afternoons and Fri morning.

P

PHOTOGRAPHY

Always ask before taking photos of people, especially women. Photographs should not be taken of any police, airports, harbours, military personnel/buildings or even inside the Madinat Zayed Gold Souk. There are several photo shops in the city that can quickly download your shots onto disk and print pictures.

POLICE

Traffic police strictly enforce the law, especially the zero-tolerance approach to drink-driving. Call 999 after any accident or incident and the police will alert the relevant service. The Abu Dhabi Police HQ is on Al-Saada Street, emergency tel: 800 1000; in Al Ain, tel: 03-762 0597. There is also a dedicated tourist police line on tel: 02 512 7777. Reporting a crime or theft can be time-consuming due to the paperwork involved, but you will always be courteously treated.

POST OFFICES

The Emirates' postal system, known as Empost, generally works very well. Main post offices such as the one next door to the Madinat Zayed Gold Souk in Abu Dhabi City (tel: 02-632 2383) and the one at Al Ain (tel: 03-7540777) are open Sat–Thur 8am–8pm, except holidays. Smaller branches are generally open 8am–3pm. All incoming mail is collected from post office boxes at one of the main post offices. Stamps can be bought from post offices and some shops but allow seven days for airmail to Europe and the USA. For more information, see www.emiratespost.ae.

PUBLIC HOLIDAYS

There are two types of official holiday when government offices and banks are closed, secular (fixed) and religious (variable dates). The dates of the Islamic holidays move forward roughly 11 days every year with the Islamic calendar.

The fixed holidays are:

1 January **New Year's Day**

2 December **National Day** (lasting two days)

The religious holidays with variable dates are:

Al-Hijra Islamic New Year

12 Rabul Awal Birthday of Prophet Mohammed

Lailat al-Miraj Celebrates the Prophet Mohammed's mystical night journey

Eid al-Fitr The Minor Feast celebrates the end of Ramadan for three days

Arafat Day Celebration of Haj pilgrimage

Eid al-Adha The Grand Feast commemorates the sacrifice of Abraham (four days)

R

RELIGION

Islam is the official religion. Emiratis and most migrant workers are Muslims, observing Islamic traditions and practices, mainly of the Sunni branch. Friday is the holy day of the week, when the majority of shops and businesses close, at least in the morning. Non-Muslims cannot visit mosques, apart from the Sheikh Zayed Grand Mosque.

Many non-Muslims work in Abu Dhabi and are free to worship at their own services, as long as this does not interfere with or contradict Islamic beliefs. The area around Al-Saada Street in Al-Mushrif in the centre of Abu Dhabi Island is home to some churches. St Joseph's Roman Catholic Cathedral (tel: 02-446 1929, www.stjosephsabudhabi.org) has daily masses in English, plus others in French, Arabic, Urdu and Malayalam. Around the corner is the smaller St Andrew's Protestant Church (tel: 02-446 1631, www.standrewauh.org), which has English services on Friday and Sunday mornings. Also nearby is St George's Orthodox Cathedral (tel: 02-446 4564), centre of the Christian community from Kerala in South India. In Al Ain is St Mary's Catholic Church (tel: 03-721 4417, www.stmarysalain.com).

T

TELEPHONES

The international code for Abu Dhabi and the UAE is +971. The local code is 02 for Abu Dhabi City, 03 for Al Ain and 04 for Dubai. All hotels offer direct-dial international services from your room, but this can be expensive.

Mobile phone service in Abu Dhabi is excellent, but using your mobile phone from overseas can be quite expensive due to high roaming charges. If you intend to use your mobile a lot or stay in Abu Dhabi for some time, buy a local pay-as-you-go SIM card (with a local UAE number) for cheaper rates. There are just two local telecoms operators: Etisalat (www.etisalat.ae) or Du (www.du.ae). SIM cards are available from pretty much any mobile shop in the country, including official Etisalat and Du outlets; you'll need to have your passport and a photocopy of the page with your photo on. Credit can be recharged using widely available scratchcards. Costs are roughly the same for both networks, but if you intend to travel outside of the main towns, Etisalat tends to have greater coverage.

TIME ZONES

Abu Dhabi is four hours ahead of GMT with no daylight-saving time:

New York	London	**Abu Dhabi**	Sydney	Auckland
3am	8am	**noon**	5pm	7pm

TIPPING

A 10 percent 'service fee' is included on most bills at restaurants, bars and hotels, although this won't necessarily go to whoever has been looking after you, so you may like to leave an additional tip to make sure they get some reward for their service. A tip of a further 10 percent should be adequate in restaurants, while hotel porters, taxi drivers and fuel attendants at service stations will also appreciate a gratuity of a few dirhams.

TOILETS

Around town there is generally no problem using the toilets in any restaurant, coffee shop, hotel or service station. Carrying tissues or toilet paper is always a good idea, especially on longer journeys.

Where is the toilet? **Wayn al-hammam?**

TOURIST INFORMATION

The Abu Dhabi Tourism Authority (tel: 02-444 0444; toll-free within the UAE 800 555; international toll-free number +971 2 666 4442; email: info@visitabudhabi.ae, www.visitabudhabi.ae) is the official tourist board of the emirate. The authority has several international offices including:

UK: 1 Knightsbridge, London SW1X 7LY, tel: 020-7201 6400, email: uk@tcaabudhabi.ae.

Australia: Level 11, 117 York Street, Sydney NSW 2000, tel: 02-8268 5533, email: australia@tcaabudhabi.ae.
USA: Trump Tower, 22nd Floor, 725 Fifth Avenue, New York, NY 10022, tel: 212-338 0101, email: usa@tcaabudhabi.ae.

In Al Ain, Jahili Fort has leaflets and information about the historic and archaeological sites around the city.

TRANSPORT

Taxis. The best way to get around the cities and towns is in an official taxi (mostly the newer silver vehicles with yellow roof signs, although a few older white and gold vehicles with a green roof sign can still be seen). All are metered (3.5 Dhs flag fare, then 1.77 Dhs per km; fractionally more expensive from 10pm–6am, when a minimum fare of 10 Dhs also applies), although some drivers may prefer to negotiate a fixed fare in advance. Taxis can be booked by phone via the TransAD hotline on tel: 600 535353 for a 3 Dhs surcharge. It can be a struggle finding the right address, so get as much information as possible about local landmarks.

City buses. An efficient and cheap bus network runs 24hr. A single journey costs around 2 Dhs per kilometre but cash is currently not acceptable.'Hafilat' (Bus) Smartcards are available at bus stop ticket vending machines, in bus stations, and in the DMA Customer Service in Al Maqta (Sun–Thur 8.30am–3.30pm). The front seats are reserved for women. For more details including route maps and timetables, see www.ojra.ae. Bus A1 leaves for the airport every 30 minutes in peak hours and every 60 minutes outside peak hours.

Inter-city buses. The main bus station in downtown Abu Dhabi has bus connections to a number of towns within the emirate and also north into the other emirates. Buses to Al Ain run every 30 minutes, and there are around five departures daily to Liwa (bus X60), taking around three hours. There is also a useful bus (X87) departing twice daily, connecting to the ferry for Dalma. A fast and comfortable service to Dubai runs every 30 minutes. Tel: 800 55555 for latest timetable information.

Ferries. The only public ferry service that can be used by visitors is from Jebel Dhanna across to Dalma Island. The vehicle ferry crosses Sat – Thur at 9am, 1.30pm and 6pm, with returns at 6am, 11am and 3pm meaning that you have to spend at least one night on the island. On Fridays it crosses at 10am and 6pm returning at 7am and 3.45pm. The additional fast 7am hydrofoil services for foot passengers are often cancelled. You may also wish to explore Abu Dhabi city from a waterborne perspective using the Jalboot ferry service (www.jalboot.ae).

V

VISAS AND ENTRY REQUIREMENTS

Entry visas are required for all nationalities (except other GCC states), and passports must be valid for a minimum of three months.

Visitors from most European Community countries, plus USA, Canada, Australia, New Zealand, Japan, Hong Kong, Malaysia, Brunei, Singapore and South Korea are issued free 30-day 'Visit Visas' automatically upon arrival, extendable for a further 30 days. Citizens of other countries should liaise with their first night's hotel, which can arrange visas for a fee. Israeli passport-holders are banned from entering the country. For full details of the various visas available, check the Ministry of Foreign Affairs website (www.mofa.gov.ae, and click on the 'Consular Services' link).

Pornography must not be brought into the UAE, and there are severe penalties for attempting to import illegal drugs. There are also bans on several drugs that are sold legally in other countries, including all cough medicines containing codeine. If in doubt, check with your nearest UAE embassy or consulate before travelling.

W

WEBSITES AND INTERNET ACCESS

Downtown areas have a few internet cafés, but these are sometimes hidden away on backstreets or upstairs. Internet business centres are found at all hotels, while there are WiFi hotspots in many hotels, offices, coffee shops and other locations. Rates per hour for internet access vary greatly.

Websites with good information about Abu Dhabi include:
www.visitabudhabi.ae – official website of the Abu Dhabi Tourism Authority.
www.abudhabi.ae – the Abu Dhabi government website.
www.tdic.ae – website of the Tourist Development and Investment Company, which is in charge of new tourist developments.
www.adnec.ae – National Exhibitions Centre website.
www.tcaabudhabi.ae – Abu Dhabi Tourism and Culture Authority.
www.ead.ae – Environment Agency website.
www.abudhabi.alloexpat.com – ex-pat community website with plenty of information and forums.
www.thenational.ae – English-language newspaper website.
www.uaeinteract.com – website run by the National Media Council, with lots of interesting information about the country.

WOMEN TRAVELLERS

Abu Dhabi is a conservative society, and female visitors are likely to encounter few problems, so long as the accepted codes of dress and behaviour are observed. For minimum hassle, wear long, loose-fitting clothing, and avoid poorly lit streets and non-tourist areas at night.

A woman alone at a beach, or one of the lower-end pubs, bars and nightclubs, can sometimes attract unwanted attention. These places tend to be well patrolled by security men or police, to whom any complaints should be directed. If you have problems with anyone, raise your voice in protest and make people aware that you might be in danger.

RECOMMENDED HOTELS

Most hotels are located in and around downtown Abu Dhabi City, although an increasing number are now opening elsewhere in the city, particularly in the Bain al Jessrain ('Between the Bridges') area close to the Sheikh Zayed Grand Mosque, where you'll find several of the emirate's swankiest places to stay. Most hotels are geared towards business guests, but as tourist numbers increase, the larger hotels are becoming destination resorts in themselves, offering a vast range of services, activities and recreational facilities. One thing to be aware of is the number of major chain hotels in Abu Dhabi City: simply telling a taxi driver that you are at the Hilton or Rotana can be confusing. Make sure you say the Hilton Baynunah or Beach Rotana, for example, to avoid problems.

The establishments in Al Ain, Mirfa and Jebel Dhanna are also mainly reliant on business visitors, but all are attractive destinations for short trips too. Liwa Oasis and Sir Bani Yas Island are the most interesting locations for tourists seeking adventures off the beaten track with a luxury hotel at the end of the day.

The prices below are for a double room, including breakfast and all government taxes:

$$$$	over 1,500 Dhs
$$$	1000–1500 Dhs
$$	600–1000 Dhs
$	up to 600 Dhs

DOWNTOWN ABU DHABI

Al Diar Dana $ *Corner 7th and 10th streets, Tourist Club Area, tel: 02-645 6000,* www.aldiarhotels.com. Perhaps the best of the various Al Diar hotels in the area, the Dana is rather dated, but in a very central location and with competitive room rates. There are 112 standard, comfortable rooms over 15 floors, with a grill bar on the top floor. It can get noisy at weekends and the food isn't great, but there are plenty of good restaurants nearby.

Al Maha Arjaan by Rotana $ *Hamdan Street; tel: 02-610 6666;* www.rotana.com. If you are in Abu Dhabi for more than a week or two, the Al Maha may be the answer. Located conveniently close to the centre of town as well as the Corniche, it offers serviced studio apartments and suites at excellent prices. Apartments come with their own kitchen and washing machine, and some boast good views of the city to boot.

Al Manzel Hotel Apartments $$ *Off Sheikh Zayed the First Street, near Al-Salam Street, tel: 02-644 8000,* www.almanzel-hotelapartments.ae. A striking glass building with 216 rooms, in a good location just down from Abu Dhabi Mall. The large rooms with kitchens are ideal for longer stays, with all the shops and restaurants that you could wish for on your doorstep. Small but pleasant swimming pool.

Asfar Hotel Apartments $ *Al-Salam Street, opposite HSBC building, tel: 02-645 7333,* www.asfarhotels.com. Suitable for long or short stays, with 54 one- and two-bedroom furnished apartments in a 10-floor building. There is a gym and business centre, but no restaurant, although there are many good eateries nearby.

Beach Rotana $$$$ *Tourist Club Area, tel: 02-697 9000,* www.rotana.com. Large resort next door to Abu Dhabi Mall, set on the waterfront behind a modest sliver of sand. There are over 500 sea-facing rooms and suites, plus a dive and watersports centre and a superb selection of 11 great restaurants and cafes including Finz (seafood), Indego's (Indian) and Prego's (Italian). A popular choice for events of all sizes, with 21 function rooms.

Ramada Abu Dhabi Downtown Hotel $$ *8th Street, opposite Abu Dhabi Municipality, Tourist Club Area, tel: 02-659 7666,* www.ramada.com. In a very central downtown location, this smart modern hotel is one of the city's standout budget options. Rooms are furnished in cool contemporary whites and browns, while facilities include a decent pool and assorted dining options complete with a couple of karaoke rooms and the Sura Asian and international bar-restaurant, claiming to have the longest list of wines anywhere in the city. Superb value.

Emirates Palace $$$$ *West Corniche Rd, tel: 02-690 9000,* www.emiratespalace.com. One of the world's most opulent places to stay, regularly hosting royalty and world leaders in its 92 sumptuous suites and 302 rooms, all with personal butler. Reputedly the most expensive hotel ever built (at $3 billion) the Emirates Palace is spectacularly designed from the sweeping driveway through to the amazing domed foyer, all with 1.3km (1 mile) of sandy beach, and two vast pools equipped with waterslides and chutes. Other facilities include nine spectacular restaurants and the largest auditorium in the Middle East, hosting top international concerts. WiFi throughout.

Hilton International Abu Dhabi $$$ *Corniche, Al-Khubeirah, tel: 02-681 1900*, www3.hilton.com. One of the city's older five-stars, in an open parkland area at the end of the Corniche towards the Emirates Palace – kids will love the Hiltonia Beach Club and the private beach across the Corniche from the hotel. There is great evening entertainment, with live music at the Jazz Bar and Hemingway's and 10 restaurants, including the ever-popular Royal Orchid Thai.

Intercontinental $$$$ *Bainunah Street, tel: 02-666 6888*, www.intercontinental.com. Large five-star on the quiet west side of town, with 444 rooms spread over 19 floors overlooking its own marina and spacious sandy beach. There is always plenty going on in the restaurant and bars in the evenings, including live Brazilian/Latin bands at Chamas, or just chill out with the smart set in the chic Yacht Club.

Jumeirah at Etihad Towers $$$$ *Corniche Rd West, tel: 02-811 5555*, www.jumeirah.com. Another hotel by the leading Dubai hotel chain, occupying one of the five futuristic skyscrapers of the landmark Etihad Towers development. The luxurious rooms come complete with state-of-the-art mod-cons, particularly good for business travellers, while leisure facilities include three pools, a private beach, the serene Talise spa and plenty of top-notch cafés and restaurants including Observation Deck at 300, the highest viewpoint in the city.

One to One Hotel – The Village $$ *Off Al-Salam Street, below Haza bin Zayed Street, tel: 02-495 2000*, www.onetoonehotels.com. Near the end of the bridge that leads to the developments on Reem Island,

The Village is just outside the traditional downtown and Tourist Club areas, but handily placed in an expanding zone that is a bit easier to access when coming to and from the airport. There are 128 rooms and good dining facilities including the outdoor Village Club, popular with families for BBQs.

Le Royal Méridien $$$$ *Sheikh Khalifa Street, tel: 02-674 2020,* www.royalabudhabi.lemeridien.com. Classy five-star, catering to both business and tourist crowds. It is not actually on the waterfront, although the spacious courtyard gardens and pool compensate, and there's an excellent selection of restaurants including the revolving Stratos at the top of the 27-storey tower, plus sunset and dinner cruises aboard the hotel's Shuja Yacht.

UPTOWN ABU DHABI CITY

Park Rotana $$ *Off Al Salam St, near Khalifa Park, Al Matar, tel: 02 657 3333,* www.rotana.com. Five-star close to the Sheikh Zayed Mosque with slick and spacious modern rooms, a good selection of places to eat and drink and a big pool. It is particularly well set up for business travellers, and prices are very competitive given the standards – although you're a bit of a drive from downtown.

Premier Inn Capital Centre $ *Abu Dhabi Capital Centre, opposite Abu Dhabi National Exhibition Centre, tel: 02-813 1999,* http://global.premierinn.com. Well-run modern chain hotel, offering very comfortable lodgings at bargain-basement prices complete with free in-room WiFi, pool and in-house restaurants and bar. The only drawback is the slightly inconvenient location, unless you are headed to the ADNEC exhibition centre, which is right next door.

YAS ISLAND

Radisson Blu $$ *Golf Plaza, Yas Island, tel: 02-656 2000,* www.radissonblu.com/hotel-abudhabi. One of a cluster of hotels to have sprung up on Yas Island – perfect if you're visiting Ferrari World, Yas Waterworld or just fancy staying somewhere away from the city rush. The stylish modern rooms boast superb views over the island and surrounding waters, plus free WiFi and flat-screen TVs, and there's good food and wine in the Filini Italian restaurant downstairs.

Yas Viceroy Abu Dhabi $$$ *Yas Island; toll free reservations tel: 888 622 4567,* www.viceroyhotelsandresorts.com. Even if you can't afford to stay here, it's worth checking out the exterior of the Yas Viceroy, built right over the Grand Prix track and next to the swanky marina – it's particularly magical after dark, when the sweeping roofline lights up with thousands of fairy lights. It is also a fine place to stay at any time, with cool modern rooms and a superb selection of restaurants, while outside of Grand Prix time rates are often surprisingly affordable.

MAINLAND ABU DHABI CITY

Al-Raha Beach Hotel $$$$ *Al-Raha Corniche, tel: 02-508 0555,* www.danathotels.com. Five-star boutique hotel with 110 rooms set behind a fine stretch of beach and palm-studded gardens, and with great views of the coast and spectacular Aldar HQ circular skyscraper. Rooms are plushly furnished and there is good nightlife on offer, including live music at the Black Pearl Piano Bar and top DJs at the Enigma nightclub. It is some way from the city centre, but conveniently close to the main highway to Dubai, Yas Island, ADNEC and the international airport.

Fairmont Bab al Bahr $$$$ *Khor al Maqta, Between the Bridges, tel: 02 654 3333,* www.fairmont.com/abu-dhabi. Supercool contemporary five-star in a prime waterside opposite the Sheikh Zayed Mosque, with striking modern design inside and out and top-notch facilities including a nice strip of private beach, the suave Marco Pierre White Steakhouse and Grill, and the posey Chameleon cocktail bar.

Shangri-La Hotel and Resort $$$$ *Qaryat Al Beri, Between the Bridges, tel: 02-509 8888,* www.shangri-la.com. One of the most beautiful places to stay in Abu Dhabi, with stunning Moorish decor and wonderful waterfront views across to the Sheikh Zayed Mosque. This hotel is as lavish in its own way as the Emirates Palace, although on a much more intimate scale. Facilities include several excellent restaurants, the top-notch Chi spa and a kilometre-long beach (with five pools), while all the shops and other amenities of the Souk Qaryat Beri are right next door. It is some distance from the centre, but well positioned for the ADNEC Exhibition Centre, airport and Sheikh Zayed Mosque.

Traders Hotel $$ *Between the Bridges, tel: 02 510 8888,* www.shangri-la.com/abudhabi/traders. Mid-range offshoot of the nearby Shangri-La, with lots of funky, colourful decor and a superb waterfront setting next to the Souk Qaryat Beri – all at very affordable rates. The neat modern rooms come with good city views and free internet and there are lots of places to eat in the adjacent souk and Shangri-La – albeit not much choice in the hotel itself.

AL AIN

Danat Al Ain $$$ *Al-Niyadat Street, Kuwaitat area, tel: 03-704 6000,* www.danathotels.com. Long-running hotel (formerly the Inter-Continental), a few kilometres from the centre out past the Hilton. It's looking a bit dated now, although the spacious palm-studded gardens (with three large pools) remain as attractive as ever, and there's a decent spread of in-house facilities and restaurants, including the popular Luce Italian restaurant, usually one of the liveliest in town.

Hilton $$$ *Al-Sarooj District, tel: 03-768 6666,* www3.hilton.com. This hotel has been a feature of Al Ain life for so long that the road from the city centre is still referred to as 'Hilton Road'. When it opened in 1972, it was the first international hotel in the UAE. It remains a popular business hotel and the centre of Al Ain social life, especially Paco's Bar for Tex-Mex food and beer.

Mercure Grand Hotel Jebel Hafeet $$$ *Jebel Hafeet, tel: 03-783 8888,* www.mercure.com. If you fancy somewhere a bit different, then this is for you. Perched at the top of Jebel Hafeet mountain, the dynamic sharp angles of the hotel tower over the jagged spurs below. The 124 rooms all lead into the great atrium, at the foot of which is the coffee shop and access to the surrounding terraces. Cafés, terraces and pool areas all have magnificent views down the mountainside and across the desert. Sunset and evening are the best times to sit out with a refreshing drink high above the twinkling lights of the city. Magical.

Rotana $$$ *Sheikh Zayed Road, off Al-Jahili roundabout, tel: 03-754 5111,* www.rotana.com. The smartest hotel in Al Ain, and also the most central, just a couple of blocks from Clock Tower roundabout. Rooms are spacious and attractively furnished, while the five-star facilities include attractive gardens and pool plus several good restaurants – the lively Trader Vic's French Polynesian restaurant and bar, with live music most nights, is always kicking.

LIWA

Liwa Hotel $$ *Mezaira Town, tel: 02-894 8000,* www.almarfapearl hotels.com/liwa. This former guest palace of the local sheikh is a great laid-back base for exploring the oasis and for 4x4 adventures into the desert, beautifully situated on top of a large sand dune just outside the main town of the oasis, with wonderful views towards the Empty Quarter desert. Accommodation is in a range of rooms and villas, and there's a nice pool, Ayurveda centre, attractive restaurant and the cosy Al-Misyal Bar.

Qasr al Sarab Desert Resort $$$$ *Liwa Oasis, tel: 02 886 2088,* qasralsarab.anantara.com. Seen for the first time, this spectacular desert resort looks like some sprawling traditional mud-brick city rising out of the untamed sands of the Empty Quarter desert – a magical sight. Close up it still manages to look surprisingly authentic, despite the five-star-plus trimmings. Camel safaris, desert walks, horse-riding, falconry displays and mountain biking give you the chance to get out into the surrounding dunes, while there's a soothing Anantara spa and stunning freeform infinity pool to unwind in afterwards.

MIRFA

Mirfa Hotel $$ *Mirfa, tel: 02-895 300,* www.almarfapearlhotels.com/mirfa. Old-fashioned resort hotel set back behind the white-sand beach across the creek from the main town, with all rooms overlooking the sea. The central restaurant is at pool level, while the adjacent Sports Pub and Lounge is the social hub of Mirfa. The hotel also serves as headquarters of the annual Al-Gharbia watersports festival each May.

JEBEL DHANNA

Danat Resort Jebel Dhanna $$$ *Jebel Dhanna, tel: 02-801 2222,* www.danathotels.com. Large seven-storey block spread across the seafront with 1km (0.6 miles) of pure white sand and warm shallow waters. Rooms all come with sweeping sea views, and there are also some private waterfront villas right on the beach. Activities include watersports and safaris around the Sir Bani Yas Island wildlife reserve.

Dhafra Beach Hotel $$ *Jebel Dhanna, tel: 02-801 2000,* www.dhafrabeach.danathotels.com. Slightly more downmarket sister hotel and neighbour to the Danat Resort Jebel Dhanna, built in the style of a single-storey desert fort. Rooms are set along the private beachfront, fringed with palms, and there is live music on weekend evenings in the Hana Bar, plus the Al-Dhafra golf links next door.

SIR BANI YAS

Desert Islands Resort and Spa $$$$ *Ruwais, Sir Bani Yas, tel: 02-801 5400,* http://desertislands.anantara.com. A beautiful hotel situated on a remarkable island. Originally planned as a guest palace of Sheikh Zayed on his royal island reserve, the building was left unfinished when the ruler died in 2004. Converted into a traditional-style hotel with wind-towers, the Anantara management now run it as a wildlife tourism destination like no other. There are five types of rooms, suites and villas to suit your taste and pocket, and as much activity as you can handle, including wildlife game drives, mountain-biking, nature treks, game trails, sea-kayaking, scuba-diving and snorkelling. If all that activity leaves you drained, perk up with the free espresso machine in each room and browse through the books in the private library. Weekends are busiest, with flights bringing guests direct from Abu Dhabi City.

INDEX

POCKET GUIDE

ABU DHABI

Third Edition 2017

Editor: Kate Drynan & Helen Fanthorpe
Author: Chris Bradley
Head of Production: Rebeka Davies
Picture Editor: Tom Smyth
Cartography Update: Carte
Update Production: AM Services
Photography Credits: Abu Dhabi Tourism Development and Investment Company 8R, 40; Alamy 19; Chris Bradley/Apa Publcations 4MC, 4ML, 4TL, 5T, 5TC, 5MC, 5M, 5MC, 5M, 6TL, 6TL, 6ML, 7M, 7T, 7TC, 8L, 9, 9R, 11, 14, 15, 16, 23, 28, 29, 30, 31, 33, 34, 36, 37, 38, 39, 43, 44, 46, 48, 50, 52, 53, 54, 55, 56, 59, 61, 62, 65, 66, 68, 70, 72, 74, 76, 78, 80, 82, 84, 87, 88, 91, 93, 94, 96, 98, 99, 100, 103, 104, 106; Getty Images 4TC, 12, 26; Leonardo 7M; Mary Evans Picture Library 20; Shangri-La Hotels 6ML; Shutterstock 6MC; TopFoto 24
Cover Picture: Shutterstock

Distribution
UK, Ireland and Europe: Apa Publications (UK) Ltd; sales@insightguides.com
United States and Canada: Ingram Publisher Services; ips@ingramcontent.com
Australia and New Zealand: Woodslane; info@woodslane.com.au
Southeast Asia: Apa Publications (SN) Pte; singaporeoffice@insightguides.com
Hong Kong, Taiwan and China: Apa Publications (HK) Ltd; hongkongoffice@insightguides.com
Worldwide: Apa Publications (UK) Ltd; sales@insightguides.com

Special Sales, Content Licensing and CoPublishing
Insight Guides can be purchased in bulk quantities at discounted prices. We can create special editions, personalised jackets and corporate imprints tailored to your needs. sales@insightguides.com; www.insightguides.biz

Printed in China by CTPS

Contact us
Every effort has been made to provide accurate information in this publication, but changes are inevitable. The publisher cannot be responsible for any resulting loss, inconvenience or injury. We would appreciate it if readers would call our attention to any errors or outdated information. We also welcome your suggestions; please contact us at: berlitz@apaguide.co.uk
www.insightguides.com/berlitz

CERAMICA
de
SANTANYI
TALLER
ARTESA
METRO
NIC W SRODKU

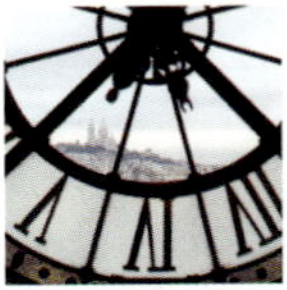

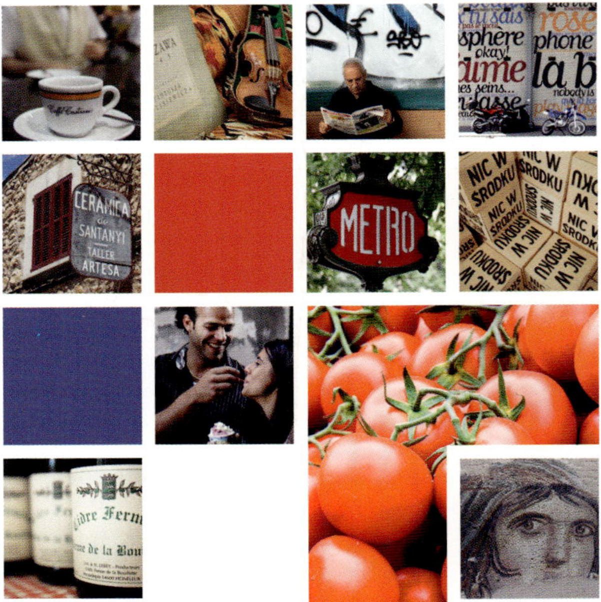

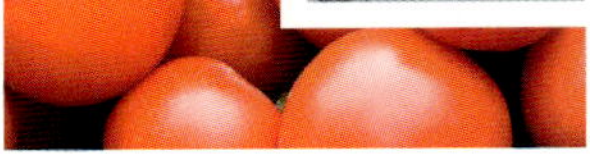